GREAT SPEECHES
FROM EUROPEAN DRAMA

GREAT SPEECHES FROM EUROPEAN DRAMA

Translated and edited by
Robert David MacDonald

OBERON BOOKS
LONDON

First published in this collection in 2002 in association with
the London Academy of Music and Dramatic Art by
Oberon Books Ltd (incorporating Absolute Classics)
521 Caledonian Road, London N7 9RH
Tel: 020 7607 3637/Fax: 020 7607 3629
e-mail: oberon.books@btinternet.com

A catalogue record for this book is available from the
British Library.

ISBN: 1 84002 002 4

Cover design: Joe Ewart

Cover photograph: John Haynes

Printed in Great Britain by Antony Rowe Ltd, Chippenham.

INTRODUCTION

The concoction of an anthology can, with fatal ease, become infected with both self-indulgence and self-satisfaction, both probably inseparable from the compiler's liking for the passages in question, nevertheless feelings, which, along with others of an even more doubtful nature, can cloud his judgment, especially when it is a question of his own work. The only defence I can offer for my present contribution to this dangerous genre is that it was commissioned – asked for? suggested at any rate – by LAMDA, behind whom I take grateful shelter.

That said, I still find myself at something of a loss to put a name to the purpose of this book. The brief was, and the title remains, *Great Speeches from European Drama*, but beyond that I can discern no cohesive factor. There is no consistency of period, type, or even length. The only things common to all these bleeding gobbets is that they were in most cases written for, and in all cases performed by, the Citizens' Company of Glasgow over a period of thirty years between 1970 and the end of the century, which, in presenting a generation of humankind, makes as convenient a place to call a halt as any.

But we are not yet out of the wood; assuming that, out of the three hundred and something productions mounted by the company over the period we are considering, a selection can be made which is both practicable and entertaining. How best to present it? Chronological order would here be as meaningless as alphabetical. Order of performance would show little more than the taste of the management changing over the decades, a matter of scant interest in this case; this is not, or only marginally, a history of the Citizen's Company. Best, then, to proceed on the principle of letting one thing lead to another, in the hope that, by the end, the ground will somehow have been covered.

Robert David MacDonald
London 2002

CONTENTS

CHINCHILLA

by Robert David MacDonald

About the first speech I am happily in no doubt, as it was specifically asked for at the first discussion of this collection. I therefore make no apologies for flagrant self-quotation. It ends the first act of my play *Chinchilla*, loosely and inaccurately based on the life and career of Diaghilev.

During a hot afternoon at the Venice Lido, quarrels are simmering among the leading figures of the ballet company; suddenly Chinchilla (Diaghilev) interrupts, decisively.

CHINCHILLA: I have now kept silent for a considerable time, while I allowed myself to be screamed at by a bunch of treacherous harpies whom I had hitherto erroneously supposed to be my closest friends, and I am now going to make a speech, of some length, and I hope, more clarity. I wish never to have to make it again, so you had better listen.

We are five people who have known each other since before we all started dying our hair. We have gone through trials and tortures that make the cellars of the Cheka look like a sanatorium, just as we have known pleasures which would make the ecstasies of Saint Francis seem a mere faint itch. And we have laughed – alone – at each other – all the time. We, together and apart, found so much in a scruffy and debilitated world, so much that was enchanting, so much that made us so happy, that it was literally beyond our powers to keep it to ourselves. Everything in life leaves a taste which we want to recall and pass on. But, with the exception of Liovka and his little paintbox, not one of us has the slightest talent for doing so. Gabriel can make money quicker than most people can forge it. Ilya can keep people together when most other people would be glad if they could keep them apart. Mimi is a supreme catalyst who can further human relationships without sacrificing an iota of her character. And I? I wanted to be an opera singer – my teacher said: 'With a voice like yours, you should have been a composer.' But none of us could *in himself* show others just what it was made the world so appetising. Chance, perhaps, threw us in the way of one another, and together we found a way to rid ourselves of a desperate inaction, as frustrating as it was futile, like nailing custard pies onto trees.

And we work. We make revolutions, we make fashions, we make scandals. Many reasonable people are appalled, many despicable people delighted, but none of that matters. It comes from us. It is a passion, a disease, a lust. Art can rest on sinister foundations, and has the most intimate knowledge of sickness. They are both the products of excess, and there is nothing anyone can do about that. The single-minded concentration of the artist works like a cancer, and passion absorbs utterly. Passion for reform, passion for power, passion for beauty; a thirst to show, a lust to tell, a rage to love. It is the only voice we can still trust in a complicated, expensive world. And because it is all too ecstatic, absurd, miserable, happy, horrible and holy to contain within myself, I will show what I love, and tell what I love, with ardour, style and impeccable bad taste, whether it is Utopia, or the death of kings, or simply those beautiful young men without whom my life is as dry as a hollow nut; so that for a moment we can see them, created in our image, in the glare of arc lamps, as we should; beautiful, clever, wise, just and alive, and for that moment forget that we are ugly, crass, guilty, foolish and dying.

Available in *MacDonald, Plays One: Webster, Summit Conference, Chinchilla,* published by Oberon Books Ltd.

ISBN: 1 870259 25 4

FIGARO

by Pierre-Augustin Caron de Beaumarchais

In the same season as *Chinchilla* (1976/7), indeed in repertoire with it, the company performed Beaumarchais' *Figaro*, a conflation of *The Barber of Seville* and *The Marriage of Figaro*, excising the, to me at any rate, tiresome Marcellina sub-plot, along with a lot of rather verbose excess baggage – even if the jumps caused by cutting necessitated a certain amount of equally excessive, if less excusable verbiage of my own.

The political subversiveness that made Napoleon remark that "*The Marriage of Figaro* is the revolution in action" and that he would have had trouble-makers like the author locked up, seems pretty small beer nowadays, particularly in this country, where such teeth as the play may still retain have been effectively drawn by the better-known opera. But Beaumarchais avoided, for his play, the transient fate of most politically inflammatory pieces, by making it deal with the one area of politics familiar to all of us, regardless of birth or fashion, namely the family.

Figaro's big speech, about the inequities of privilege, was divided into two, the first part serving to introduce the leading character, the second bringing the argument round to his being the wronged husband-to-be.

FIGARO: Lindoro! What's in a name? The most unreliable things in the world: change them as often as you will, the object will stay more and more the same. A gentleman in love may behave like a madman, but calling himself something else does not permit him to behave like a clown. Well, if we protected all fools from their folly, the world would be fuller of them even than it is. I have pulled His Lordship out of enough scrapes before now to warrant pushing him into one in the end. What is this longing to exchange liberty for servitude? The man whispers "My angel", the woman coos "mama, mama", and two idiots are persuaded they think alike: the slave loses everything in his chains, even the desire of escaping from them. Still, money will hide many faults, and an ass loaded with gold gets to the top of the castle. With money, every man is wise, handsome, and sings well. All the same, I had rather have a crown in my pocket than on my head – it is the only hat that will not keep out the rain. In search of money I have buzzed about the world these thirty odd years, here, there, everywhere and nowhere. The child of God knows who, raised in the street, I aspired to the drawing room and an honest living: but all my studies, in chemistry, surgery, pharmacy would get me was a place as assistant to a horse-doctor. At sight of my lancet, the sickest nag grew well, and I found myself without employment. Unsure of my identity, I decided to turn it to advantage and went into the theatre, where I wrote a play attacking a fallen minister, who returned to power the day of the first performance, and I found myself an unwilling guest of the State. My visit concluded, there remained nothing but theft. Seeing that all men were equal at the card-table, I opened a gambling-den, only to discover that while everyone stole from each other they expected me to be honest. On an impulse I withdrew from the world, and a few feet of water were near to making the rupture definitive, when a beneficent Heaven recalled me to my senses, and my former state: I took up my razor once more, and leaving glory to the fools who grow fat on it, and shame to people with horses to carry it, I went from town to town, a free man at last. Still, if I cannot get money for myself, perhaps I can help His Lordship to love, and who knows, some of both may rub off on me in the process. Keep things moving, I say – rust wastes more than use.

In between this and the second part of the speech, the Count makes his marriage, with Figaro's help, and under his cynical observation, ending the first part of the play to the satisfaction of most of those involved. Resuming the action four years later, the Countess reflects on the problems of maintaining such a state as marriage. In the middle of the night, a clock strikes, as she enters in a nightgown.

ROSINA: I thought I heard voices. Midnight has sounded and Lindoro does not come. How many midnights now since last he came to me? How many more must I lie awake and listen to the clocks ticking and striking my life and looks away? Loss, infinite loss of all, but of love most of all: where Hunger does not conquer Love, Time must and Time will.

Oh, to have neither mirrors nor memories – I would still believe myself eighteen. But no – I am four years married, and instead of lying still in that great world which was the circle of Lindoro's arms, here I wander each night through this deserted castle, stopping the clocks one by one, to tell me it is not too late. But it is: tomorrow my maid Susanna will marry Figaro, and all those others whom my husband pursues will marry, and at last, their children will point at me behind my back and whisper "Look, there goes the old Countess Rosina!" And their mothers will pull them back and scold them, and pity me, but tears dry soon enough when shed for others.

Clock strikes one.

Again! I must go in. Oh, Lindoro, I am like an expensive, jewelled watch that hangs always at your side, but is never wound up. Your oaths were big as the sky, as you said you would love me until lamps ran on cold water. But I have lost your love, and still they run on oil.

Her attempts to relight her husband's love lead her inevitably into a misunderstanding involving him and Figaro. Any attempt at a synopsis of the plot of the last act would be as thorny – and as futile – as trying to describe how to tie a bow tie without diagrams. Here is Figaro again, suspecting the Count of betraying him with Susanna.

FIGARO: All my assurance was nothing but a blown-up balloon. One little pin pricks it for ever. I see why he was so put out about the fireworks. Well, if I'm married enough to have the right to be angry, I'm not so far married that I can't marry someone else. Oh, woman, woman, weak, disappointing creature…no animal can be untrue to its nature – is it yours to deceive? In the very middle of the ceremony, to send him, under my very nose…and he smiled as he read it, while I stood by like a block. Well, my Lord Count, Commander of the Fleece, Chamberlain of cape and sword, Grandee of Spain…with all of this, you shall not have her. Because you are a great nobleman, you think you are a great genius…birth, fortune, rank, position: how proud they make a man feel! What have you done to deserve all this? Put yourself to the trouble of being born, no more. For the rest – a very ordinary fellow. Whereas I, born into the crowd, have had to deploy more knowledge, more talent, more calculation, more skill, merely to stay alive, than has been needed to rule all the provinces of Spain for a century. And you would measure yourself against me, would you? Great weights hang on thin wires, Your Lordship.

PHEDRE
/BRITANNICUS

by Jean Racine

The step from, arguably, the most famous French comedy, the first that could be called modern, to the most famous of French tragedies, was a step that took the Company a decade to accomplish.

Nations tend to be proprietary about their great tragedies, denying other nations the ability, let alone the cultural stature, to perform them adequately. Reflection might indicate that comedy was more difficult to export across the Channel, but theatre managers axiomatically and immemorially dictate that comedy is more attractive, on a programme at any rate, than tragedy – and so a myth is perpetuated.

In Racine's *Phèdre* ideas of "Honneur", "Gloire", "Sang", and the like, are concepts with which the British actor may not be familiar, and may therefore have trouble expressing. Think of Falstaff's peroration on Honour and imagine its specific elaboration in French.

Here is Phedra, finally confessing her love for her stepson to her appalled nurse, Oenone.

OENONE: What cruel fate lay here in ambush, waiting for
　　Our unsuspecting landing on this perilous shore?

PHEDRA: My sickness has an earlier origin. My Lord
　　And I were tied in marriage; all things seemed assured;
　　My peace, my happiness...suddenly in the crowd,
　　I saw my enemy, disdainful, hostile, proud.
　　I turned to him, turned pale, turned red and turned aside.
　　I felt confusion rising; my mind stupefied.
　　I could not speak or breathe; things swam before my eyes;
　　All through my body ran at once both fire and ice.
　　I felt the presence of the Goddess, and those fires
　　That burn our lineage with insatiable desires.
　　I sought to turn her rage aside by dedication,

Temples were built to her, months lost in decoration.
Victims were sacrificed each day, a holocaust
In which I tried to find the reason I had lost.
Offerings made in vain, pretences of belief,
Cures powerless to relieve a love past all relief;
I invoked the Goddess, spoke her name aloud, in vain;
Only the name Hippolytus ran in my brain.
Seen through the reeking haze of sacrificial flame,
I made my offering to a god I dared not name.
I studied to avoid him. Then…the worst disgrace;
I saw him, only him, in his own father's face.
At last I forced myself to wound him, to rebel
Against my deepest feelings, make his life a hell.
To rout the enemy whom I loved more than my life
I played the wicked stepmother, the second wife.
I urged his banishment from Athens, and attained
My object: he was sent away, and I regained
Some of my former calm, and for a little while
I felt relief to know him safely in exile.
Submitting to my duty, I raised the children of
My marriage, hiding all the tell-tale marks of love.
Pointless stratagems: fate, cruel and unforgiving,
Made Theseus bring me to this place, where *he* was living.
I saw my exiled enemy: a stab of pain
Tore at the half-closed wound and made it bleed again.
The fire's not hidden in my veins where none can see:
The Goddess, clawing at her prey, possesses me.
My life became a horror to me and my passion
Something I could not bear to think of. Reputation
Was all I thought about, and so I longed for death
To bury my dark secret with me in the earth.
I could not watch you suffer. Your distress, at last,
Drove me to tell you all. I shan't repent what's past;
Only respect my longing for it all to end;
And do not try to fan the last remaining fire
From dying embers. Let them die – as I desire.

*Hippolytus' appalled reaction on learning of this drives her further
in her admission, if only to prevent him leaving the room.*

PHEDRA: I have revealed too much for 'misinterpretation';
    You see me stand before you torn apart by passion.
    I am in love. Guiltless in my own eyes, my love
    For you is not a thing of which I can approve.
    It was not cowardice or compliance bred the poison
    Of the insane desire that now destroys my reason.
    Venus has sought me out for her revengeful curse;
    You may abhor me, but I loathe myself far worse.
    I call the Gods to witness, those cruel Gods, that flood
    My loins with fire, like all those of our cursed blood;
    Gods who seduce weak human beings, as they please,
    From the straight paths of love to perverse heresies.
    I tried to fly from you, but it was useless. Malice
    And desperation made me drive you from the palace.
    I sought your hatred; it alone could strengthen me.
    What was the upshot of my futile strategy?
    You loathed me all the more, I did not love you less:
    Your grace and beauty only grew in your distress.
    I pined in tears, shrivelled in fire, past remedy;
    You could have seen, if you had ever looked at me.
    What have I said? Can you imagine I enjoyed
    Confessing shame I tried expressly to avoid?
    Take your revenge on me and on my love together.
    Show yourself the son of your heroic father,
    And slay another monster, the most dangerous,
    Theseus' wife that dared to love Hippolytus!
    Only this monster sees its death as a reward;
    Here is my heart; here is where you must sheathe your
                          sword.

    Kill me. Or, if I'm thought too vile an enemy,
    Should your hate begrudge me so sweet an agony,
    Or if your hand would be defiled by such foul blood,
    Then do not plunge it in yourself – give me the sword.

In a play bristling with 'great speeches', the temptation to over-quote is hard to control, but it would be perverse to omit the speech which French schoolboys have to get by heart, and which French actors endlessly prepare for auditions, the récit de Theramène, *the tutor's monologue describing the death of Hippolytus.*

THERAMENE: We'd scarcely left the city, passing the
                                    fortress gate,
He riding in his chariot: his stricken guards
Drawn up around him, like him, at a loss for words.
Following the shore-road, brooding, he neglects
The reins, left loosely dangling round his horses' necks;
While they, whom formerly he only could control,
Now hang their once-proud heads like nags, their dull
                                    eyes roll,
Catching his sombre mood with that same sympathy
With which they would respond to him in days gone by.
And then it happened. Suddenly, a dreadful cry
Seemed to rise from the sea-bed, up to split the sky;
Then from the centre of the earth another voice
Groaned out in answer to that first appalling noise.
Our hearts all turn to ice. The blood clots in our veins.
The horses are alerted. The hair stands up on their manes.
Now the flat surface of the water seethes and boils;
A wave, high as a mountain, rears up, approaches, falls
Crashing upon the shore, and spews, in the eddying surf,
A monster such as never has been seen on earth.
Half-bull, half-dragon, horned, with leprous yellow scales,
Its body coiled around in tortuous fetid trails.
Bellowing, lurching forward, it shakes the troubled shores;
The winds shriek in the sky in horror at its roars.
The earth heaves: venom and disease hang in the air;
The very wave that cradled it recoils in fear.
All flee, rather than bravely make a useless stand,
And seek asylum in the temple near at hand.
All but your hero-son. He grabs his javelin,
Wheels his team round, and while we stand there marvelling,

Rides on the beast, takes careful aim with steady hand,
Inflicting in its flank a gaping bloody wound.
Howling in pain and rage, the horror leaps and falls
Down at the horses' feet, roaring, writhing in coils.
Its gaping gullet vomits out a sickening flood
That overwhelms them all, of fire, smoke and blood.
The horses panic, there's no halting their career,
And neither rein nor rider do they heed or hear.
Their master wastes his strength; they cannot be subdued:
The bits between their teeth are creamed with froth and
                                        blood.

In this confusion many say they saw a god
Stabbing the maddened chargers with a fiery rod.
Stampeding towards the rocks, fear gave them impetus;
The axle screamed and snapped. Fearless Hippolytus
Sees his chariot fly in matchwood, ruined, mangled;
He falls himself, in harness helplessly entangled.
Forgive my grief. The sight is one that I shall see
Through every second of what life is left to me.
I saw, my Lord, I saw your most unhappy son
Dragged by the stallions he'd trained, fed, ridden on.
He shouts to halt them, but they panic at the sound.
His whole sweet body soon is nothing but a wound.
Our shouts of desperation echo all around.
At last their panic ebbs, their energy runs down.
They halted not far from the ancient sepulchres
that house the dry bones of his royal ancestors.
I ran there, breathless, his guards panting at my back;
His blood had left a terrible but easy track.
The rocks were drenched with it; thorn bushes everywhere
Dripped red with dreadful traces of his blood and hair.
I called: he held what once had been a hand to me,
Opened his dying eyes, closing them instantly,
And spoke: 'I'm innocent. The Gods decree this end.
I leave Aricia in your care, my old, dear, friend.
And if, one day, my father should be disabused
And mourn the murder of a son falsely accused,

If he should ever wish to appease my memory,
Tell him that he should treat his prisoner leniently,
And give her back her…' At that word, his spirit fled,
And I held nothing but a body, mangled, dead.
Sad victim of the victory of the Gods, he lies,
Whom even his father could no longer recognise.

While still with Racine, there is surely room for something from Britannicus, *though this is the only example here of a script not translated specifically for Glasgow, but for the Almeida Theatre in 1998. Based on historical rather than mythological figures, it has a more down-to-earth tone than* Phèdre *though the elevated language that permeates all of Racine is still there, for example in Agrippina's catalogue of her machinations in favour of Nero, her son.*

AGRIPPINA: Nero, come over here, sit down and take
                                    your place.
    They summon me to clear myself with you, here, face to
                                    face.
Though what I am accused of, I, of course, have no notion,
But of those crimes I did commit, I owe some explanation.
You rule. But I'd remind you just how wide a gulf
There was, at birth, between the Empire and yourself.
My forebears' rights and claims could give a guarantee
Of nothing – things would have stayed so – but for me.
The moment Britannicus' mother was condemned,
Battle was joined for the prize of Claudius's hand,
You think I coveted his bed? My one desire
Was to ascend the throne, so as to raise you higher.
I enlisted the help of Pallas – yes, I swallowed my pride;
Night after night I lay, the Emperor at my side,
Fondled in his arms, and nourishing the love
That I, his niece, had fought to be so certain of.
But we were joined in blood, and the age-old taboo
Of incest barred the way to marriage for the two
Of us. He dared not wed Germanicus's daughter,
His niece. But the Senate was seduced, and brought a
Milder law into force, Claudius to my bed,

And all Rome to my feet – however, it must be said,
The honours they bestowed were not for you, but me:
I had you brought into the bosom of his family –
And more than that. Tying us closer still, I gave you
In marriage, to his only daughter, to Octavia.
But that was not enough. Could I, or anyone,
Think Claudius would prefer his son-in-law to his son?
Once more I went for help to Pallas. By his persuasion
Claudius adopted you. To celebrate the occasion,
He named you Nero, planned to share supreme authority,
Though you were still a few years short of your majority.
That was the moment everyone recalled my past...
Unmasked my plan. But I was steady. I held fast.
Murmurings were heard; the Emperor's friends could all
Begin to sense Britannicus's coming fall.
I made them promises, bought off most of them,
And exile spared me from most of the worst of them.
Claudius, tired out with endless complaints from me,
Dismissed from his son all those whose constancy
And loyalty had too long been given to him alone,
And might still beat a pathway for him to the throne.
And I did more. I chose from my own retinue
Those whom I wished his education entrusted to.
While, on the other hand, for you I took good care
To pick out tutors whom Rome would certainly revere.
Deaf to intrigue, I listened only to reputation,
Brought Seneca back from exile, Burrus from his station
In the army. Both of them have since...but never mind,
Rome was much impressed with their virtues – at the time.
Meanwhile, I handed out largesse, in your name, in amounts
Sufficient to exhaust the imperial accounts.
Circuses, honours, gifts, by whose seductive charm we
Could win the people's hearts, and more than that, the army.
By now the Emperor's health had rapidly declined.
Claudius' eyes had long been closed, as had his mind.
They opened now. He saw his error. In his fear,
The glimmerings of pity for his own son appeared.

He hoped, too late, to reunite his allies, as a whole.
But his guard, his bed, his palace, were all in my control.
I let him fruitlessly consume himself in sighs,
Then made myself the mistress of his last energies.
Ostensibly to spare him grief, as he lay dying, I hid
From his all knowledge of the tears his son had shed.
He died. A thousand rumours blackened my reputation:
I kept all news of his death out of circulation,
While Burrus went in secret to the soldiers to demand
The garrison's renewal of allegiance to you, and
While you went to the camp, following my desires,
The altars of all Rome smoked with sacrificial fires.
Following my false orders, the populace obeyed
With fervent prayers for the health of a prince already dead.
Only when your rule was ratified by the legions'
Approval, and their oath of absolute obedience,
Was Claudius shown to them; Rome learned of your
                                                    accession
And his death at the same time. There is the confession
I promised I would make you. Those are my crimes, my
                                                    lord,
Without omission or exception. My reward?
For six short months, with seeming gratitude, you appear
To enjoy the resultant fruits of so much tender care,
Now, tired of showing respect that irks you, like a sore,
You think you can affect not to know me any more.
Burrus and Seneca I saw, giving you welcome lessons
In rank ingratitude, poisoning you with suspicions,
So pleased to see their pupil outstrip their arguments.
I've watched you bestowing royal marks of confidence
On worthless flatterers, voluptuaries, rakes,
Pandering to your pleasures for their own worthless sakes.
And when I could no longer contain my indignation,
When I asked you at least for some proper explanation,
You gave me a reply of the most insulting sort.
(The ungrateful, when exposed, fall back on that resort.)
You know I promised Junia in marriage to your brother.

They both expressed delight at this choice of your mother.
And what do you do? You abduct her. Overnight
She is made the passive object of your obscene delight.
Octavia is forgotten, banned from your heart and head,
From where I took such pains to place her, in your bed.
Pallas, I hear, is exiled, Britannicus arrested,
And now, my freedom is attacked. Well, who was it
                    suggested

Burrus be allowed to lay insolent hands on me?
And when you are convicted of so much perfidy,
When I require from you some adequate explanation,
I am the one who is summoned to plead in justification.

Or in the 'messenger-speech' of the nurse, Albina, at the very end of the play.

ALBINA: The emperor is condemned to an unending sorrow.
  She is not dead, she – where Nero may not follow.
  When she escaped from here, she ran as if to go
  To see Octavia, but then she took a road
  That leads to nowhere. I watched her as she ran, distraught,
  Out of the palace gates. She soon found what she sought,
  The statue of Augustus. Falling down, she wept
  At the marble feet, her arms around him, prayed: "Accept
  My prayers, Prince; by this cold stone that I embrace,
  Protect, both now and henceforth, the last of all your race.
  Rome has just seen the murder of the only one
  Of all of us who worthily could have called himself your
                    son.

They wished me to betray him after he had died.
But I must keep faith with him. So I here decide
To dedicate myself to that eternal god,
Whose altar you now share, your virtue's just reward."
Meanwhile the people, by the confusion worse confounded,
Press on her from all sides, until she is surrounded
By a multitude, that, moved by her tears, and pitying
Her obvious distress, take her beneath their wing,
And lead her to the temple, where they still maintain,

As in ages past, the eternal Vestal flame.
Nero sees all of this, but does not dare to enter:
Narcissus, more intent to please, makes for the centre,
Approaching Junia, fearlessly, with utter lack
Of shame, begins, profanely, to try to force her back –
A blasphemy that falls victim to a hundred blows:
His sacrilegious blood incontinently flows,
Drenching Junia. Nero, barely comprehending
What he is looking at, abandons him to his bloody ending –
And goes back. All avoid him. Silent, grim,
Junia's name the only sound that comes from him.
His walk is aimless, he seems not to dare to raise
His eyes to heaven, with their distraught, unsteady gaze.
When night falls on his loneliness, people begin to fear
That circumstance might sharpen the agony of despair
If any longer we refuse him our assistance,
His grief is such that he may show death no resistance.
Time presses. Hurry! The slightest anxiety for your son
Could make him kill himself.

AGRIPPINA: And Justice would be done.

The drawback with Racine is that, once you start quoting, there seems no cogent reason to stop.

Available in *Britannicus*, published by Absolute Classics, an imprint of Oberon Books Ltd.
ISBN: 1 84002 083 0

THE GOOD-HUMOURED LADIES
/DON JUAN

by Carlo Goldoni

It was around the time of *Figaro* and *Chinchilla* that the company first programmed a play by Carlo Goldoni (1707-1793), who was to become an unofficial house author, represented by fifteen plays, more than any other writer. *Mirandolina* (1976) opened the series, as a stopgap for a cancelled production, and proved successful enough to be followed next season by the marathon *Country Life*, and, at the Edinburgh Festival of 1979, by *The Good-Humoured Ladies*, and, at the Venice Biennale the following year, on Goldoni's home ground, at the Teatro Goldoni indeed, by *The Battlefield*. Finally we had clocked up a grand total of fifteen productions, a considerable advance on the collected playhouses of the country, and possibly of Europe outside his own country, during the same period.

Goldoni suffers from the opposite drawback to Racine: where the one is eminently, endlessly quotable, the other is not. Goldoni seldom writes a speech of more than four or five lines, unless he is compelled to explain a twist of plot, and his dialogue, though puzzlingly buoyant, is for the most part naturalistic to a fault. Even so, there are exceptions.

Here, from The Good-Humoured Ladies, *a representative stock character of the* cavaliere servente, *a sort of licensed escort for married women, delivering to two of the ladies of the title, a disquisition on his condition.*

CAVALIERE: Love, like the priesthood, must be a vocation,
    And servitude a full-time occupation:
    Save that the service of the Deity
    May possibly afford more cause for gaiety
    That can be found among the love-lorn laity.

    What must Love's soldier do, when he enlists,
    And takes his fortune in his puny fists?

Forsake his friends, all company forbear,
In case the Fair One should have time to spare –
A moment's joy, bought with a month of care.

The galley-slave of love must kiss his chain,
Smile when she rattles it, and not complain:
Insult and injury endure and pocket,
Mock his own passion, and let others mock it,
Even at risk of being thought a blockhead.

Rivals he must endure, at her mere whim,
Though *she* may take them, merely to vex *him*:
And though his jealousy consume him quite,
Though he may sigh by day and weep by night,
He ends by owning she is in the right.

And if she lights upon another man?
He must stand calmly by and hold her fan,
And hold his tongue, however high the cost,
Nor put on vengeful airs, nor make riposte,
In hope thus to regain what he has lost.

For him who can accept such punishment,
Farewell the tranquil mind, farewell content!
For him who cannot grovel *and* adore,
Caress the whip, and beg her still for more,
Simply farewell! His occupation's o'er.

Thus far the poet penned, and I append
A sharp conclusion for a bitter end.
In love the victors from the vanquished fly;
They flee that wound, and they pursue that die.
I must make clear though, to the unobservant,
I here protest myself, your humble servant.

Like so many playwrights, Goldoni felt impelled, albeit at the beginning of his career, to write a Don Juan play, keeping more or less to the standard plot, which crystallised in Da Ponte's version for Mozart, though, as Goldoni himself pointed out, "for the first time without any supernatural intervention". His Don is very much a

figure of the Enlightenment, the century of Casanova and de Sade.
Here he is, at the feet of the Comendador's memorial statue, justifying
his behaviour in his death to Don Alfonso, a courtier.

DON JUAN: I say, Señor, the face of Donna Anna
    Blinded me – seduced me; I took fire
    At those fair eyes, and to the fire of love
    Was added an indulgence, as unwise
    As it was liberal, in the pleasures of
    The table; an intemperance – unworthy
    Of a noble soul! Oh, the unhappy chalice
    Of two perfidious gods, Cupid and Bacchus!
    I blush to tell you; but I must not hide
    The truth from you, for, at that fatal moment,
    So utterly did desire supplant my reason,
    I was no longer master of myself.
    Ah, what unlucky star compelled my host
    To quit the table, leaving me alone
    And ardent at the side of so much beauty?
    My burning heart interpreted the event
    Prompted by its desires: I boldly asked
    The fair one for deliverance from my torment.
    She answered with contemptuous modesty;
    Her rage lit up a further fire in me.
    Reason by now had fled me; and my fury
    Carried me on to threats. At this sad juncture
    Her father entered, armed, deaf to excuses –
    He challenged me. I, under provocation,
    Gave blow for blow, governed not by my will,
    But by a cruel fate, which brought my sword
    Fatally to his breast. He fell, transfixed.
    There, Señor, are my faults: I have confessed them.
    Remember, though, that I was blindly led
    By two blind, traitorous gods. If we could just
    Free from this stone the fallen hero's voice,
    Might it not plead for mercy for me now?
    Perhaps he now repents not having curbed

His overpowering rage, perhaps he would
Condone in me a wild excess of youth.
What use would my death be to him? What use
My blood to his reluctant, grieving daughter?
To remedy his injuries, he should ask
For something else from me, something whose justice
I hardly could deny, my hand in marriage
To her who, through my fault, is now in mourning.
If Don Juan dies will Donna Anna's honour
Be thereby restored? Will she allow
The world to harbour doubts of whether she
Defended her honour from a resolute lover
Successfully, or did she fight in vain?
Poor Donna Anna! Overborne by grief,
She does not see the greatest of her dangers.
I go too far – I know. The criminal
Cannot prescribe the punishment for his crime.
However, is it not legitimate
To ask for pity, just as it is to make
Such sacrifice as will restore the damage
Without the loss of blood? Ah, Don Alfonso,
Speak you for me. You can obtain for me
The royal clemency, and Donna Anna
Will be rewarded with my hand, while you,
Though losing one friend, will have gained another,
Less valorous, I grant, but no less faithful.
Be my protector. Not from love of life
Am I urged now to ask your charity,
But love of blood, and care for reputation.
The mercy of the great King of Castile
Is known to all the world, as is his justice.
May he not now give an example of it,
Which will both profit him and do him honour?
It is not the punishment of a crime for which
The world reserves its wonder, but the clemency
Of a merciful monarch, since the world is full
Of wretched crimes, but poor in merciful kings.

The persuasiveness of this speech is considerable, and only vitiated by the sudden appearance of Donna Anna, demanding vengeance. Juan rouses himself to new efforts.

DON JUAN: Pity, Donna Anna, is what I ask.
    I am at your feet; on you depends
    My life no less than my dishonoured name.
    You wish to see me dead? Here is my breast,
    Take a sword – run it through. You will the better
    Relieve your rage, and I at least shall die
    Without the shame of public punishment.
    Remember it was love that blinded me,
    And your fair eyes that first set me on fire,
    And that to see you, to be near to you
    Alone and unobserved, and not to languish
    And ask for charity would be impossible.
    To a man driven desperate by your refusals,
    Who could apply a curb or give advice?
    Your father challenged me at a sad juncture...
    I can say nothing to excuse my crime.
    I am guilty, I confess, and I should die.
    You do not see me throw myself before you
    To save my wretched life. Ah, all I ask,
    For pity's sake, if pity is in your heart,
    Is that you show some scrap of kind regard,
    If not to the life, at least then to the honour
    Of a lover who has been unfortunate.

He then offers her his hand in marriage, in the style of Richard III wooing Lady Anne, and she comes to within an inch of accepting him, only an opportune denunciation from the king preventing Juan from making his escape. For his last scene he is in the guard of Carino, a shepherd boy engaged to one of his victims.

DON JUAN: Better I should invoke the horrid furies
    Of Hell, that they should come to tear my body.
    For a man facing despair beyond all doubt
    Pity is useless, useless all advice.
    I must die, but let Death come himself to fetch me.

What Fate reserved me for so harsh an end?
Cruel, barbarous mother, to give me life!
Unfeeling nurse, not to cut off that life
Of treachery while I was in the cradle!
Oh, let me curse the day when I was born!
The vicious feelings nourished in my heart!
Donn'Anna, Elisa, Donna Isabella!
Which of you is it that will murder me?
Then do it, shepherd… Here I am at my end;
Disarmed, a captive, wracked with cruel hunger,
And crueller anger. Comendador, where are you?
Will you not take revenge for your own blood?
Will your fine effigy not fall on me,
And carry me down below the earth? Why not?
Could I, once more, before I die, transfix
That breast of yours! False, pitiless deities,
I defy the avenging power of your arm.
If it is true there is a Heaven above,
If there is justice there, then send the lightning
To strike me, kill me, bury me deep in Hell
For all eternity.

Available in *Goldoni, Volume Two: Don Juan, Friends and Lovers, The Battlefield*, published by Absolute Classics, an imprint of Oberon Books Ltd.

ISBN: 1 870259 37 8

ANTONY

by Alexandre Dumas père

Another author overdue for reappraisal, and by the Citizens' Company nearly as much as any other, is Alexandre Dumas père, a power-house of energy, even if every word was not his own – but where would painters be if they could not leave details to assistants? Unlike Goldoni, who worked with a permanent company of a dozen actors, each expert in a line of parts, Dumas had neither the advantages nor disadvantages of such a position, but fitted his fifty-odd plays in between the production of huge three-decker novels, travel books, cookery books, memoirs, newspaper articles and whatnot. He is, like Goldoni, not easily quotable, and for some of the same reasons – fragmentary dialogue, with interlardings of purple patches of romantic extravagance, which require the sometimes too long runway of an overwrought situation before they can become properly airborne.

In 1831 he wrote the melodrama *Antony* and French theatre was never quite the same again.

In the fourth act, through a mouthpiece, Eugene, a dramatist, at a party, he puts the case for his method of writing plays.

EUGENE: Comedy is the portrayal of manners; Drama, of passions. The revolution made all Frenchmen equal, producing a confusion of station, a uniformity of dress, leaving nothing to indicate a man's profession: codes of manners and usage remain undefined, everything is fused together, the colours a painter needs have become shades…

…All this makes the comedy of manners, if not impossible, certainly extremely difficult of execution. There remains the drama of passion, and here we find another difficulty. History bequeaths facts to the poet, which are his by hereditary right: he exhumes the men of ages past, reclothes them in the costumes they wore, agitates them with their former passions, augmenting or reducing them according to the dramatic force he wishes to give them. But, if we tried to show the naked heart of mankind, in our unromantic evening clothes, no one would recognise it. The likeness between stage and audience would be too great, the analogy too intimate; the spectator, watching the actor develop his passions, would want to stop him at the point at which he himself would have stopped; if that passion went beyond his own powers of feeling and expression, he would fail to understand, and would say: "It is false: I don't feel it like that; when the woman I love deceives me, I suffer, of course…for a bit. But I don't stab her to death, or myself, and the proof is – here I am." Thence the accusation of exaggeration in melodrama, masking the applause of the few, who, more fortunately, or unfortunately, endowed than the rest, recognise that the passions in the nineteenth century are the same as in the fifteenth, and that the heart beats beneath a tail coat as warmly as beneath a steel cuirasse. There are only two things which finally interest the public: the True and the Big.

HIDDEN FIRES (LE CHANDELIER)

by Alfred de Musset

On being complained to by a fellow-author about how difficult it was to write plays, Dumas replied "Why write plays? It is so much easier not to write them", which is all very well, coming from as prolific a competitor as Dumas. Another way out was to write them, but not for performance, though what actually was supposed to be done with them is hard to tell. There seem to me, and I admit to speaking as a dramaturg, few more otiose occupations than reading plays. Nearly all the major poets of the nineteenth century, in England as in the rest of Europe, took this road. Browning, Shelley, Keats, Wordsworth and the rest, all of them were set adrift without a strong theatrical tradition to keep them afloat – the damage done to the English theatre by the Puritan Revolution is incalculable, worse even than that inflicted in a similar compass of time, on the German theatre by the Nazis. A few may have struck intermittently lucky, Tennyson for instance finding Irving, the actor needing the respectability conveyed by a major literary lion, and the author recognising genuine dramatic muscle when he saw it, but the theatre as a whole was as reluctant to entertain the rather hi'-falutin' notions of the literary establishment, as the literary big guns were to descend into what they must have seen as an inferno of burnt cork and red noses.

Of the contemporaries of Dumas who drew back from risking their work in the hands of the incandescent performers of the time – why is it that great dramatists and great actors so seldom coincide? – the most distinguished is certainly Alfred de Musset. Although produced in the last decade of his life, with varying success, most of his stage work has had to wait until the twentieth century to come into favour with an increasingly conscientious theatre, the result itself of state subsidy, however limited.

In 1987, the Citizen's Company produced Le Chandelier, *under the title* Hidden Fires, *from which the next speech is taken, which might, with advantage be compared to the speech from* The Good-Humoured Ladies. *Clavaroche, an officer, is having an affair with the wife of a local lawyer, and proposes a means of avoiding discovery.*

CLAVAROCHE: In the regiment, a fire screen is what we call a well set-up, good-looking lad, who is commissioned to carry a shawl or an umbrella if need be: who, when a woman gets up to dance, gravely sits on her chair, follows her in the crowd with a melancholy gaze, and plays with her fan, gives her his hand to escort her from her box, and proudly places on the nearby console table the glass from which she has just drunk. If the lady is admired, he struts like a peacock; if she is insulted, he fights. A cushion is missing on the sofa: he is the one who runs, rushes, to find it, since he knows the house and its ins and outs, he is part of the furniture, finds his way about in the dark. Is there some party, some entertainment, somewhere the lady wishes to go? He is up with the lark, shaved by dawn, down in the square reserving seats with his gloves. He accompanies her on her walks, reads to her in the evenings: buzzes around her unceasingly, besieges her ear with a rain of inanities. He plays bezique or piquet with her aunts in the evenings. As he is more than a match for the husband in diplomacy, ability and sheer enthusiasm, he soon makes himself thoroughly disliked. Ask him why he does all this, and he will be unable to tell you. It is not because the lady occasionally favours him with a smile, or, during the waltz, abandons her fingertips to him which he clutches with ardour. He is like one of those grand gentlemen who bear an honorary title, weightier far than the duties it involves, who have the entrée on high days and holydays, but to whom the cabinet is closed, such things being none of their business. In a word, his favours leave off just where real favours begin: he has everything one sees of women, but nothing one desires of them. Behind this convenient mannikin lies hidden the ecstatic mystery: he acts as a fire screen, shielding all that happens beneath the mantelpiece. If the husband is jealous, it is of him; if there is gossip, it is on his account. He is the one who is shown the door one fine morning, after the servants have heard footsteps at night in Madame's chambers; he is the one who is spied on in secret; his letters, full of tenderness and respect, are the ones steamed open by Madame's mother-in-law. He comes and goes, up and down, he frets himself, he has all the trouble, it is his place: by means of which, the discreet lover and the innocent female friend, decked with an impenetrable veil, laugh at him and at the speculations of the inquisitive.

Later, in a soliloquy in front of a mirror, Clavaroche bewails the lot of a man of quality forced to spend time in the provinces.

CLAVAROCHE: In all conscience, if one loved any of these pretty women seriously, one would be in for a fine time: the profession of a rake is all in all a ruinous and laborious one. One moment, at the pitch of ecstasy, some scullion scratching at the door sends you scuttling into hiding. The woman who is risking all for you only listens to you with one ear and in the midst of transports of delight sends you packing into a cupboard. At another moment, you're at home, stretched out on a sofa, exhausted after manoeuvres, and a messenger sent post haste comes to remind you that there is one who adores you at a distance of several miles. Quick, a barber, your valet, batman. You run, you fly: there is no more time, the husband just came back; it's raining: you are forced to cool your heels for a whole hour. Do you take it into your head to be ill, or simply out of humour? Don't think of it. Heat, cold, tempest, fire, flood, uncertainty, danger, are all there merely to keep you up to the mark. The difficulty lies, since first there were proverbs, in having the possibility of increasing the pleasure, and the icy blast of winter would be much put out if, as it cut you to the quick, it did not believe it was putting new heart into you. In truth, they paint Love with wings and a quiver: they would do better to show him as a duck-shooter with a waterproof jacket and a woolly cap to keep his head warm.

What stupid beasts men are, refusing a good tuck-in at someone else's expense, all to run after…what, for Heaven's sake? (*Going to mirror.*) But garrison duty lasts for six long months; one can't be always going to the café; provincial actors are boring; one looks at oneself in a mirror, and one has no mind to be handsome to no effect; Jacqueline has a pretty figure… That is how one learns patience, accommodates oneself to things, and doesn't make too many difficulties.

By ill fortune, the lovers' search for a fire screen brings them to one of the husband's law clerks, Fortunio, who happens also to be desperately in love with Jacqueline. A trap is set for him in the garden, which the husband is supposed to spring. Now acquainted with the whole affair, he confronts Jacqueline bitterly.

FORTUNIO: My poem? And what will you do with it, cruel woman that you are? You have been talking to me for the last quarter of an hour, and not one syllable of feeling has escaped your lips. It was all a question of your excuses, your sacrifices and reparations. A matter of your Clavaroche and his stupid vanity. A matter of my pride! Do you think you have wounded it? You imagine that what is hurting me is to have allowed myself to be taken in, and made a fool of at a dinner party. I can't even remember it. When I said I loved you, do you think I didn't feel anything? When I tell you of two years of suffering, do you think I meant it as y you would have done? Well, do you? You break my heart, you pretend to be sorry, and then you leave me like this. Necessity, you say, made you commit a fault, and you regret having done so. You blush, you turn your head

away, what I am suffering evokes your pity. You see me,
you understand what you have done, and the wound you
have given me, this is how you cure it. Ah, it is a wound
in the heart, Jacqueline, and all you need to do
is hold out your hand. I swear to you, if you had wished
it, however shameful it may be to admit it, however
much you may smile about it to yourself, I would have
agreed to anything. O God! My strength is deserting me.
I cannot leave this place.

No, keep your smelling salts. For him. Along with all
these attentions I am not worthy of: you are not paying
them to me. I do not have such an inventive wit, I am
neither lucky nor clever. I would not have been able at
need to construct such a deep stratagem. I was mad – to
think I was loved! Yes, because you smiled at me,
because your hand trembled in mine, because your eyes
seemed to search for mine and to invite me like two
angels a to a feast of joy and life, all because your lips
parted, and empty sound came from them. How
ridiculous! Was your smile congratulating me on the
beauty of my horse at the parade? Were your eyes
dazzled by the sun flashing from my helmet? I came out
of a dark room, where for two years I had been following
your walks in the garden: a wretched junior clerk who
had the presumption to suffer in silence. What a suitable
object for your affections.

You say "Poor boy!"? Then say it again, for I don't
know whether I am awake or dreaming, and whether, in
spite of everything, you do not love me. Since yesterday
I have been so utterly brought down, beating in vain my
heart and my head: remembering what I have seen and
heard and asking myself whether such a thing is possible.
At this moment, you say it is, I feel it is, I am suffering,
dying from it, and neither believe nor understand it.
What did I do to you, Jacqueline?

How could it happen, that for no reason at all, feeling
neither love not hatred for me, without knowing me,
without ever having set eyes on me: how could it have
happened that you, whom everyone loves, you whom
I have watched giving money to beggars, watering those
flowers out there, you who are good, who believe in
God, to whom it never... Ah, I am accusing you, you
whom I love more than my life! Oh, heavens! Have
I reproached you? Jacqueline, forgive me.

What am I good for, dear God, if not to give my life for
you? If not for the most wretched employment you can
make of me? If not to follow you, to protect you, to
clear the thorns away from before your feet? How dare
I complain, after you have chosen me! I had a place laid
for me at your table; I was to count for something in
your life! You were going to command all Nature to
smile as me, as you did. Your image, beautiful and
radiant, began to walk ahead of me, and I followed after.
I was going to live...and am I losing you, Jacqueline?
Have I done something for which you are sending me
away? Why do you no longer wish even to go through
the pretence of loving me?

*After this it should come as no surprise that the young man faints
dead away, before being brought back to life by a confession of love
from the lady, who dismisses her previous lover, and all ends happily
enough for most of them, which is as good an ending as we have any
right to expect these days.*

VAUTRIN

by Honoré de Balzac

A curiosity of this period, by any standards, was Balzac's *Vautrin*. Like many other novelists, Balzac nourished the illusion that the quick way for a writer to make money is to write for the stage, undeterred by what must have been the familiar sight of indigent playwrights by the dozen, then as now. It needs only one hand, and not many fingers of that, to tot up the number of writers who have made a real success in both fields – Dumas, Somerset Maugham, Sartre…any other takers?

Another illusion novelists suffer from is that writing for the theatre takes up very little time. Balzac, whatever misgivings he may have had about his capacity as a playwright, certainly believed so, but even he miscalculated. Having accepted a commission to write a play for Frederic Lemaitre, the leading romantic actor of Paris, he found himself, the day before he was to read it to the company of actors – a normal practice for authors, now unhappily discontinued, thus depriving actors of a few legitimate sniggers – forced to admit that he had not penned a word. Nothing daunted, he summoned five of his intimate colleagues, gave them the synopsis of an act each, left bottles of champagne, and locked them in, to be released only on completion of their common task. Theophile Gautier, reputed to have been one of the galley slaves, said that when he went to the reading the following morning, the play read by Balzac bore no resemblance whatever to the product of their collective toil. The legend, which is attractive enough, is probably just that – a legend. But the resulting play, although a mess, has much in it that makes it worthy of the other appearances of the great master-criminal in Balzac's novels. It was possibly using rough notes for a future novel that gave the play its initial impetus, or perhaps a discarded scenario, hauled out of a bottom drawer and chopped into shape against time. Whichever way, it provides a tremendous leading part, with multiple changes of costume and accent, several excellent supporting parts, strong situations, frustrations, lost orphans, incipient vice, young love – what more could an audience demand? A coherent plot, perhaps? Maybe, and here I found myself obliged to step in to snip off a few loose ends. It may be no more comprehensible now than originally, but at least it will withstand nit picking. I also succumbed to the temptation to tinker with some of the speeches, to the extent that, in some cases, I can no longer recall where my own contribution leaves off and Balzac's begins again. (There is also a wholesale importation of a scene from *Le Père Goriot*, which, albeit at some cost to the overall length, does clarify a portion of the play.)

Here, Vautrin expresses his somewhat limited satisfaction at the way his plans to infiltrate his protégé, Raoul, whom he has picked up out of the gutter, into the upper reaches of Parisian society, are proceeding.

VAUTRIN: After twelve years of underground labour,
I shall in a few days have conquered a great position for Raoul: I must make it secure. Ach, this wretched love affair… I wanted him to shine, by himself, subduing, by my counsel, and on my account, that world which I can never enter again. Raoul is not simply the son of my brain and of my rancour: he is my revenge.

But have I sufficiently polished, caressed the magnificent instrument of my domination? Raoul was brave and headstrong, he would have thrown his life away: I had to make him cold, positive, take away his fine illusions one by one and put him through the fine mesh of experience, make him defiant and cunning as…an escaped convict, never letting him know what I was. And now this mighty scaffolding is in danger of being torn down by love. He should have become great, and now he will he no more then happy. I shall go and live in a corner of the sun of his prosperity: his happiness will be my work. I shall be like a man, half-way up a cliff who has found a ledge where he can sit, and if he does not wish to alter his position, he will be as safe there as he would be on the top. Providing the weather doesn't change. At least I shall hear Raoul's name on every side, and I shall have the pleasure of a forger seeing his signature accepted on a cheque. One must limit oneself to what one can possess utterly, and I, and I alone, shall possess the knowledge that my temptations, my obsession, my splendours, my miseries, and he is all of these, are the envy of the world.

And this Inez? What will she possess so utterly? For the last day or two I have been wondering whether this little Princesse d'Arjoz should not perhaps succumb to a little fever…of the brain. It is inconceivable what women can destroy.

Some time later, Raoul comes within a hair's breadth of spoiling everything by challenging a rival to a duel. Vautrin decides to teach him a lesson.

VAUTRIN: And what have you undone? Twelve years of work, twelve years when I watched you asleep and awake, plotted arid schemed for you, for the moment when you could take the one thing I could not give you. And now you ruin everything, for a duel? A duel is only a ceremony now. One knows in advance exactly what will happen, even what one should say when hit. Stretched out on the damp grass, one's hand on one's heart, one speaks a generous pardon for one's victorious adversary, and an eternal farewell to some unthinking angel, who, if she is not entirely imaginary, will probably go to a ball the evening of your death, in order not to excite suspicion.

You play with your life as if it belonged to you. Oh, it is easy enough to be brave at the head of a squadron of cavalry, shining in steel: once the charge is sounded, the horses will do the rest. But when danger comes on you alone? Unexpected? Ugly? I said you would despise me,

and the cock has not even crowed once yet. What I did
was not for gratitude, but because those we love are not
like other people, made up of qualities which we can like
or reject as we wish: they are all of a piece, and any part
of them can stand effectively for the whole. I would have
had a part of you – your success would have been mine.
My life has been lived in action so that boys like you
may dream. Well, if you are to grow up, as you insist,
I will leave you your dreams, but now there is a price,
and you will not grow up until you pay it. You will
discover that the truth is not the same thing as beauty,
whatever your poets may tell you, and that the truth is
nothing to what you will have to face. No, I shall not tell
you who you are, I shall leave that to others for whom
the news may be more welcome, but I shall tell you who
I am. You have seen me in one ridiculous disguise, now
you will see me in another. I have tried to keep you in
Paradise, now eat the apple, and find out that the keeper
of the Garden and the serpent may be one and the same
person.

(*Stripping his shirt down to his waist.*) Look at my back.
What do you see? Scars. Dead flesh. Without feeling
anymore. But the scars hide other scars, that will only be
revealed through a pain greater than that which inflicted
them. You have a rope in your hand. Use it! In love we
inflict pain, if that is the price of not feeling it so much
ourselves.

RAOUL, stung, strikes him three times across his back.

Harder. Are the letters showing? You have stopped, so they
must be. Your hand rests on the brand of a criminal,
sentenced to hard labour for life. That is the honourable
source from which your fortune comes. But I shall save
you still, and from yourself.

FAUST

by Johann Wolfgang von Goethe

Goethe is a name only recently heard in British theatrical circles; partly, I surmise, from an endemic uncertainty about how to pronounce it – Go-eth? Gooth? Geeth? Goth? – and because the only theatre work of his that had been heard of in this country, namely *Faust*, was of such length that even cutting it for performance is no inconsiderable labour. But, with diligence and taking matters at a good, brisk clip, it is possible to play a consistent version of both parts in not much over three hours: I say 'both parts', since cutting things off at the end of Part One is like jumping ship before it docks – we don't even get to know whether the devil got his bargain or not.

The play starts with a pair of rather jokey prologues, one in the theatre, one in Heaven, before introducing the main character, suitably, and in this case literally, burning the midnight oil.

FAUST: Here I am then. Philosophy
    Behind me, Law and Medicine too,
    And – to my cost – Theology…
    All studied, grimly sweated through:
    And here I sit, as big a fool
    As when I first attended school
    True, I surpass the dull incompetents,
    Doctors, pastors and masters, and the rest,
    For whom there is no bliss but ignorance,
    But this pre-eminence I now detest.
    All my laborious studies only show
    That nothing is the most we ever know.
    Scruples I've laid aside, and doubts as well;
    I have no fear of the Devil or Hell –
    And this is what robs me of all delight.
    I cannot boast that what I know is right;

I cannot boast my teaching will ever find
A way to improve or to convert Mankind.
Meanwhile I live in poverty;
No dog would choose to live like me.
And so the rites of Magic I rehearse,
To probe the secrets of the Universe;
To learn its mysteries and recognise
The force that binds all Nature's energies;
To see creation's principle at work,
And waste no more time on the trade of Talk.
(…)
Imprisoned in my library
With stacks of papers ceiling-high,
Worm-eaten junk, pell-mell together hurled
With scientific instruments,
A valueless inheritance.
This is my world! Here's what is called a world!

Away with it then! Leave it all behind!
A better, secret mentor springs to mind.
From this I know there is a world elsewhere.
What other guide do I need to take me there?
Spirit speaks unto spirit and divines
The meaning of mysterious designs.
Spirits, I feel you, hovering near me;
Answer me now, if you can hear me!
(…)
I feel the strength to be my fate's defender,
To bear both earthly woes and earthly splendour,
To grapple with the storms, a worthy contender,
And in the grinding shipwreck not surrender.
The clouds close in above me…
The moon is hidden…
The lamp burns low…
Vapours rise…
Red beams flicker about my head,
And from the roof a shuddering horror

Floats down and seizes.
I feel you, Spirit I have called, you hover near.
It's tearing at, my heart. Appear!
At each new pang I feel
My senses reel…
I feel my heart surrender, gripped as in a vice…
Oh, come! Oh come, you must, though death should be
the price!

*The challenge is taken up by the fearsome Earth Spirit, whom Faust,
however, cannot control or detain…*

FAUST: But in that moment, drenched with ecstasy,
    I felt my pigmy self grow great;
    It thrust me down and sentenced me
    Once more to Man's uncertain fate.

    Am I God's image? Shall I rank with gods?
    No – I am only kin to worms and clods
    Of common clay, the pounded dust which packs
    The shelves that wall in academic hacks.
    Is it here I'll discover what I lack?
    Read through a thousand books and all to find
    Humanity puts itself upon the rack,
    And Happiness is rare among Mankind?
    What are you grinning at, you hollow skull?
    Because your brain, like mine, once sought the spark,
    Of Truth, but fell a victim to mere dull
    Confusion, and was swallowed in the dark?
    My complex instruments stand mocking me:
    To Nature's secrets you were to be the key.
    But if she will not teach her mystery,
    There's little merit in Technology.
    My father's junk, unused, inherited –
    What we can't use does nothing but impede.
    Nothing is owned unearned, unmerited:
    Necessity creates the only things we need.

What thing is that, though, which impels my gaze?
Why is that phial a magnet to my sight?
Radiance plays around me, like the rays
Of moonlight, in the forest, in the night.

In you I honour human art and skill,
Quintessence of all soothing anodynes
Which every rare and deadly power combines,
Now, for your master, all your strength distil!

Another day! A chariot of fire
Comes near. New roads lie open to me. I
Shall pierce the veil that hides what we desire,
Break through to realms of abstract energy (…)
Summon my daring to pass through the gate
That most men shun in every way they can.
Now I must show, in action, that a man
May be as free as gods, and be as great (…)
And take this step with calm determination,
Though it should bring with it annihilation.

The draught intoxicates as it is drawn.
The dark, narcotic flood streams out to fill
The cup; juice I have chosen and distilled
To be my last drink, drunk with firm soul and will,
In solemn salutation to the coming dawn!

He raises the cup to his lips. There is a clangour of bells and chanting.

Music of God, so powerful and so sweet,
Why do you seek me out here in the dust?
Go entertain the faithful, if you must,
I hear the message, but my faith is weak.
A miracle is religion's dearest child:
The Easter hymn brings childhood flooding back to me.
I must retrace my steps, be reconciled
To all that made my last step a possibility.
Ring, sing of resurrection and rebirth!
My eyes are wet: I have returned to earth.

Dissuaded, in one way or another, from suicide, Faust takes a walk with his lumpish student Wagner, through the Easter crowds, during which he sees a black dog running round them. The creature follows them home, and finally manifests itself as Mephisto, who, after some little banter hardly suitable to so momentous an occasion, sends Faust to sleep with a vision of sensual delight, provided by spirits.

MEPHISTO: Vanish you sombre
    Ceilings above us
    Scudding and fleeting
    The dark cloud no longer
    Threatening hovers
    Starlight is shimmering
    Suns of a glimmering
    Radiance greeting
    The children of light
    Who throng in the air
    Infinite longings
    Follow them there
    Their beauty covers
    The gardens where lovers
    Deep in their visions
    Lost in emotion
    Swear their devotion
    For life to each other
    Wine gushes streaming
    Foaming and creaming
    Through gemstones in fountains
    Leaving the mountains
    For lakes brightly gleaming
    Birds fly south to lightness
    The islands of brightness
    That ride on the ocean
    For ever in motion
    Where joyfully round us
    Choruses sound as
    We see them advancing
    Swaying and dancing

Some of them climbing
Over the hills
Some of them swimming
Where the sea swells
Some hovering in space
Yet all of them are
Seeking the far
Live-loving star
And its infinite grace.

At which Faust wakes, disillusioned.

FAUST: Cheated again! Was the Devil here?
How did the spirits disappear?
Was it a dream? Was it a riddle?
Was it a poodle? Or was it evil?
Here I am at the middle of the way,
Too young to be without desires, too old
To be content to throw my time away.
What comfort can the mortal world still hold?
"Renunciation: learn to do without!"
They all say – they don't know what it's about.
I wake each morning with a start of pain,
Knowing that by the time each day is done,
I shall be forced to acknowledge, yet again,
Not one desire has been fulfilled – not one.
And once again, as Night descends;
And I lie staring on my bed,
The Hell that is inside me sends
Terrible dreams to fill my head.
Deep in my soul, God stirs the springs,
But cannot move external things.
Existence is become a mere dead weight:
Would death could free me from the life I hate.

The bond with Mephisto is finally signed and Faust embarks on his new and dubious career. The first thing he does after being rejuvenated is to fall in love, something for which his previous academic career has not prepared him very well, and he behaves as appallingly as nearly everybody does. For the moment, though, the girl in question, Gretchen, is too fascinated to think ahead.

GRETCHEN: I'd give a lot if I could know
    Who that gentleman was just now.
    A gentleman he was, that much I clear,
    Or else he'd not behave so cavalier.
    How thundery and close it is tonight,
    And yet it's not exactly warm.
    I feel a sort of… I don't know…not right…
    I wish my mother was at home.
    I'm feeling nervous as a cat;
    There's nothing to be frightened at.

Singing as she undresses.

"A king of a Northern fastness,
True to the grave, it's told,
Was left by his dying mistresss
A drinking – cup of gold.

He knew no greater treasure
In all his after years,
Yet each time he drank a measure,
His eyes would fill with tears.

At last, his life declining,
He divided his kingdom up,
All to his heirs assigning,
All but the golden cup.

In the great ancestral castle,
With his knights of high degree
He sat and feasted his vassals
In his palace by the sea.

The old man stood there, drinking
His life's long last draught up,

Then, into ocean flinging
The sacred golden cup.

He stood and watched it fall, and
Fill and sink in the sea,
Then he turned his face to the wall, and
Never more drank he."

As she opens the press to put her clothes away, her eyes fall on the jewel-case.

What's this? Dear God what do I see?
I never saw such things. They're good enough
For a princess. How would this look on me?
I wonder who can possibly own such stuff?
If only some of them belonged to me,
People would look at me quite differently.
What is the use of youth and looks?
All very fine for folk in books,
But no one wants it any more:
Their praise has pity at its core.
They just want gold
To have and to hold,
That's all. God help the poor.

But more proper counsels prevail, to Mephisto's disgust.

MEPHISTO: I'd damn my soul to Hell this very minute,
Were it not for the fact that I'm already in it.
The jewels we left, which that girl should have got,
Some pestilential priest has swiped the lot!
She told her mother. Instead of saying "*Bonne chance,*
You lucky girl", she has an attack of conscience.
She has a nose for sin: you may be sure
She sniffed at once the jewels were not quite pure.
"Gretchen, my girl," says she, "ill-gotten wealth
Corrupts the mind, it's not good for your health.
So, to be on the safe side, I'll arrange a
Gift to the Church, to keep you out of danger."

Gretchen is pulling quite a face, of course,
Thinking "well, there's goodbye to my gift-horse."
Thinking besides, "How can he be
Wicked if he can leave such things for me?"
Off to the priest, however, who takes one
Look at the stuff, and says, "Child, you have done
A Christian deed, which is its own reward.
Only the Church can properly afford
Such carriers of moral indigestion.
Ladies, whole countries fall to her in forfeit,
Without her ever complaining once of surfeit.
She alone has the stomach, without question."
With which, he sweeps the whole lot off the board,
As if they had been crumbs swept off a table,
And leaves, as soon as he is decently able.
While Gretchen, in an indecisive mood,
Doesn't know what to do, or if she should.
But she's more curious than she is cross
Some consolation in her tragic loss.

*Faust, having attained the right, true end of love, now has leisure
to show his discontent with life, love and the rest of it. However
traumatic this may be, it presupposes a considerable expansion of
the play in Part Two.*

FAUST: Transcendent spirit, you have given me all
    I asked you for. All Nature and all Knowledge
    Became my province, and I had the power
    To feel it and enjoy it. Nor was it
    A mere cold, curious glance you let me take.
    You let me gaze into Nature's deepest heart
    As if into the bosom of a friend
    The ranks of all things living you paraded
    Before me, teaching me to recognise
    My kinship with all creatures, in the water,
    In the quiet thicket, in the air.
    When the storm howls and whistles through the forest,
    And the great trees fall headlong, bringing down
    Neighbouring trunks and branches, with a crash,

That echoes round the hills with hollow thunder,
You shelter me in safety, in a cave,
And show me to myself, reveal the depths
And mysteries that lie hidden in my own body.
Now the bright moon comes up before my eyes,
Bringing me peace; now there float up before me
Out of the rock face and the dew-drenched bushes
Silvery forms of lost forgotten worlds
Soothing the iron discipline of thought.

But nothing perfect ever comes to Man.
I see that now. The happiness you gave me,
Which brought me nearer to the gods, has brought me
In addition, this companion, whom already
I can no longer do without, however
Impudently and unfeelingly
He lowers me in my own eyes, and turns
Your gifts to dust and ashes without a word.
He busily fans a hungry fire of lust
Inside me for that object of desire.
I stumble from desire to consummation,
In consummation pining for desire.

*Gretchen, meanwhile, discarded by Faust, and gnawed by remorse,
prays before a statue of the Virgin.*

GRETCHEN: Mary, look down,
    Thou rich in sorrow's crown,
    Have pity on my misery.

    With pierced heart
    And bitter smart,
    Gazing on Thy son's last agony.

    Thy piteous sighs,
    To heaven rise,
    In His and Thy extremity.

    Who can see?
    My agony
    That cuts me to the bone?

My heart, afflicted,
Broken, rejected,
Is known to Thee alone.

Wherever now I go,
Such woe, such woe, such woe
Is here within unspoken.

And when alone, my fears
Bring tears, bring tears, bring tears:
I know my heart is broken.

The flowerpots in the window
Were wet with tears, not dew,
When early in the morning
I picked the flowers for you.

And early in the morning
The sun shone overhead;
But I was up before him,
In misery on my bed

From shame and death deliver me.
Mary, look down,
Thou rich in sorrow's crown,
Take pity on my misery.

Another character, Gretchen's brother Valentine, now appears, on compassionate leave, to look after his sister's now ruined reputation.

VALENTINE: Full many a drunken crowd I've been in,
    Where men would boast about their women,
    Describing, with more noise than wit,
    Their own particular favourite
    And toasting them. Meanwhile I'd lean
    Propped on my elbows, in serene
    And quiet confidence, until
    They had all talked or drunk their fill.
    Then I'd say, full glass in hand:
    "*De gustibus non disputand –*
    Um, but where in all this land'll

You find a girl to hold a candle
To my own sister, Gretchen? There is none."
Roars of assent, as everyone
Agreed she was the flower of womanhood,
Shutting the noisy boasters up for good.
And now… Each time her name is spoken,
It's matter for a dirty joke, and
Any filthy drunken brute
Can call her whore and prostitute.
And like a criminal I sit
Sweating to hear such talk, but swallowing it.
I'd like to kill them! But even if I tried,
I could not say that one of them had lied.

He challenges FAUST to fight, but MEPHISTO paralyses his sword-arm and FAUST gets in a quick and fatal thrust.

This scene is succeeded by the general chaos of the Witches' Sabbath, the flight of Faust with Mephisto, and the visit to the prison where Gretchen is now awaiting sentence for the murder of her child, and indeed of her mother. Faust begs her to escape with him, but her mind has gone.

GRETCHEN: If only we could once get past the hill.
My mother sits there on a stone –
I feel a chill of dread –
My mother's sitting there on a stone –
She nods and wags her head.
But not in sign to me. Her head's too heavy for her.
She won't wake now. She's slept too late. Before, her
Sleep made sure that we could be alone.
That was a happy time. And now it's gone (…)
Take your murdering hands off! What are you trying to do?
Time was when all I did was done for love of you. (…)
Daybreak? Yes, today. My last day dawns on me;
My wedding-day, it was supposed to be
(Tell no one you've already been with Gretchen)
My wreath, what a shame!

It's faded now.
We'll meet somehow,
But not dance again.
The crowds are gathering out there,
In silence they overflow the square.
The death-bell tolls, the rod is snapped:
Now they seize me, my wrists are strapped,
To the scaffold they drag me, violently.
On his own neck, each man can feel
The breath and twitch of falling steel.
Crack! And the world fades, silently.

Part Two opens with Faust uneasily asleep, rocked by various deities.
With the sunrise he wakes.

FAUST: The throbbing pulse of life returns to greet
    The dawn of day. The constant earth, all through
    The long, dark night was true to me: it too
    Breathes with new quickened life beneath my feet
    And rouses in me the resolve to do
    All Man can do to make his life complete.
    Now the world lies spread open to the day;
    The forest hums with multitudinous voice;
    Light's fingers probe the darkness from the sky,
    And all the myriad forms of life rejoice.
    Colour on colour separates from grey,
    And all around me here is Paradise.

    Look upward now! Already each mountain height
    Heralds the solemn hour of dawning day.
    They are touched first by the eternal light
    That only later comes to us below.
    But now the Alpine slopes are green and bright;
    New clarity, new brilliance start to show,
    Step by step, over all the countryside.
    The sun strides out! – and blinded by the glow,
    My eyes shot through with pain, I turn aside.

So is it, when a long-held hope aspires,
Trusting, to the goal of its desires,
And finds fulfilment's door stand open wide,
When, suddenly, from the eternal depths inside,
An overpowering flame roars to confound us.
We wished to light the torch of Life – and look!
A sea of fire – such fire! – washes all round us
In giant, sweeping tides of pleasure and pain.
So that we look down to the earth again,
To shelter in youth's – Spring's – everlasting cloak.

Then let the sun stay always at my back!
Down precipices roars the cataract.
I watch it, with growing wonder and delight,
Crashing from fall to fall, to join and split,
In a thousand torrents, hurling up spray and foam
And suddenly, nobly, rising from the storm,
The rainbow bends, in colours ever-shifting,
Now clear and bright, then in the heat-haze drifting
To spread its fragrant coolness everywhere.
There is the metaphor for the human story:
Reflected on, the meaning's crystal-clear;
Our life is brilliant, but reflected glory.

He and Mephisto proceed to the Emperor's palace, where they make themselves generally, if rather sinisterly, agreeable, solving, among other problems, the bankruptcy of the Empire by inventing paper currency. The courtiers express their satisfaction variously – here a drunkard celebrates...

DRUNKARD: Nothing can disturb my pleasure,
Not today, I feel so free.
Happiness in tuneful measure,
That's what I have brought with me.
And I keep on drinking, drinking,
Come! Drink up there! Glasses clinking
At the back there, everyone!
Raise your glasses, drink it down.

Though my wife gave me a ragging,
Sneering at my motley coat,
Took me down peg for bragging,
Called me "Fool" and "Drunken goat",
Still I kept on drinking, drinking,
Kept those beaded bubbles winking.
Fools and drunken goats, come on!
Raise your glasses, drink it down.

Let them call me addle-headed:
Here's where I shall spend my life.
If the landlord won't give credit,
Try the daughter or the wife.
And just keep on drinking, drinking,
Clink your glasses till you're stinking.
Everyone to everyone,
That is how things should be done.

Here and now I satisfy
Pleasures that come to my hand.
Where if all, there let me lie,
Since I can no longer stand.
Brothers, keep on drinking, drinking,
Keep those glasses clinking, clinking.
I shall meet you all anon,
Under the table, where I've gone.

Mephisto soon spirits Faust off to another world, that of classical mythology, where Faust seems more at home than the devil, who here shows his confusion at the multiplicity of mythological sorceresses, and their ability to change shape and disappear at the wrong moment.

DEVIL: Wandering round this fiery field, I've been
    Disgusted and repelled by what I've seen.
    Most of them naked, the odd shirt at most,
    Sphinxes, giant ants, gryphons, a shameless host
    Of all manner of creatures, winged and hairy,

Offering back and front views to the unwary.
Although, like all the rest of you, I find
Perpetual solace in a dirty mind,
I cannot stomach the lack of ambiguity
With which these things were treated in antiquity.
Today, we like such things, however quaint,
To be treated with some style and more restraint. (…)
Though I know how to manage Northern witches,
I'm none too happy with these foreign bitches.
At home, though things mayn't look as nice as this,
At least one knows exactly where one is.
But here! At any moment, how d'you know
The ground won't rear up suddenly from below
A mountain – maybe not what the Swiss would call
A mountain – nevertheless quite tall
Enough to block the Sphinxes from my view.

Enter the LAMIAE.

What's this attractive, if disorderly crew?
The curse of Man since Adam's time still lies
On us. We all grow old – but who grows wise?
The hallmark of the human race is
Tight corseting and painted faces.
All these once knew of good, they have forgot:
Touch them, their limbs well nigh fall off with rot.
We know it in our bones, yet still we prance
Like puppets – when the carrion pipes, we dance (…)
I shall press ahead, and not
tangle in the web of Doubt.
If there were no such things as witches.
Who'd be in the Devil's britches?
(…) Though the light is pretty dim,
You seem not unprepossessing,
nor too dear for my possessing
really quite attractive creatures,
with some most unusual features.

(...) I'll have the little one over yonder!
Damn! Changed to a six-foot anaconda!
Well, then, the big, tall one might do all right.
Changed to a broomstick! This is not my night.
There is the plump one: yes, I see
A genuine possibility.
Soft, firm and chubby, just the sort of piece
To fetch a good price in the Middle East.
Third time lucky! Let me at her!
Devil take it, an empty bladder!
Much wiser I am not, that much is clear.
The north's absurd, but no more so than here.

Much later, Faust, by now a hundred years old and immensely rich and successful, as many become who give up on love, is engaged in an elaborate scheme of land reclamation, to make new Lebensraum for the human race – parallels with Hitler's actions in Russia should not be seen as coincidental. Abetted by Mephisto, this involves Faust in the forced eviction and murder of two old people, Philemon and Baucis. Lynceus, the all-seeing watchman, witnesses the incident.

LYNCEUS: For vision begotten,
    For watching employed,
    My oath unforgotten,
    The world I enjoyed.

    I saw what was far,
    I saw what was near,
    Moon, planet and star,
    Stream, forest and deer.

    In all things I saw
    I found endless delight,
    And delighted, the more
    That they ravished my sight.

    Oh, fortunate creature,
    Such things I have seen,
    Whatever the future,
    How fair it has been!

But I do not watch up here
For pleasure only. Listen! Sounds
Of threatening horror, cries of fear
Come from the darkness all around.
Sparks of fire I can see, flaring
From the orchard's double night;
Fanned by winds, the flames are glaring
Now with even fiercer light.
Now the cabin is ignited;
The mossy roof begins to burn.
The aged couple trapped inside it
Do not know which way to turn.
No rescue for the poor old folk,
So good, so generous, so kindly –
In the midst of fire and smoke,
They are left to perish blindly,
All is now a mass of flame,
The hut a charred and blackened frame.
Now the chapel's set alight
And collapses with the weight
Of fallen, flaming branches – why
Am I cursed with my all-seeing eye?
All dies down to a cinder glow
And goes out. It is over now.
Those sights that gave delight and ease
Are one now with the centuries.

Carried away by his vision of fulfilment, Faust, now blind, after a visit from Care, proceeds inevitably to the fulfilment of his blood-bond with Mephisto.

FAUST: The clang of pick and shovel cheers my soul.
My conscript labourers toil ceaselessly
To set the earth's new, wider boundary,
And bring the ocean under our control:
A limitation firm and rigorous. (…)
Overseer! Use every means you can –
Recruit more workers, draft every healthy man:

Press-gang them, or if you have to buy them,
Pay what they cost. If they won't come, shanghai them.
Bring daily bulletins, which indicate
New work laid out, and current progress rate. (...)
Along the mountain range is all marsh ground
Infecting all that we have so far done;
To drain that festering latrine would crown
My life's work – my last triumph would be won.
I shall give living space to untold millions
To live free, active lives in affluence.
Green fertile fields, where men and herds
Can live at ease upon the new-won earth,
Settling on the solid, firm-set hill,
Built by a bold, industrious people's skill.
Here within a Paradise – outside
Up to the very margin boils the tide,
Gnawing its way through: when it does so, each
And every man combines to mend the breach.
Though there's still danger. Life and liberty
Are theirs alone who fight for them each day.
Hedged round with perils, here a man could spend
A worthy life, from childhood to the end.
I see a race grow, fearless, self-reliant,
Living their lives out here, proud and defiant.
Such a race of men I long to see,
Standing upon free soil, a people also free.
Then to the fleeting moment I could say:
"You are so beautiful – can you not stay?"
Through all of Time, the achievement of my day
Upon this earth will never pass away.
I sense foreknowledge of such happiness
And now enjoy my highest moment – this.

But Mephisto has not won, despite appearances. The last scene brings hosts of angels against him, who finally find the way into his heart, hitherto impervious to sexual temptation, by sending a boy angel to tempt him, and while he is thus distracted, they make off with Faust's soul.

MEPHISTO: You call us damned, and look at us askance:
    You are the sorcerers *par excellence*. (…)
    (This is a terrible experience.
    Is this the elemental power of love?
    I am on fire, and yet I hardly sense
    The flame that I've become the victim of.)

    Come down to earth a bit: that serious style
    Quite suits you, but I'd love to see you smile.
    Just raise the corners of your mouth; that's how
    It's done – and look a bit less virtuous now.
    There's too much modesty about that dress;
    What's underneath is anybody's guess;
    You could with decency wear rather less.
    Don't turn away now! oh, even in retreat
    The rascal still looks good enough to eat.

Pulling himself together.

My devil's nature's reassured;
The dose of love was quickly cured.
Doused are the fires of temptation,
A curse on all to mark the occasion.
Mephisto's himself again!

The ANGELS soar up, bearing the immortal part of FAUST.

What's this? Where's the rascal gone?
You've done me, young as you may be!

The cage is open and the bird is flown.
You little devil! you've made a fool of me.
You smuggled my prize out on the sly
And filched my legal property.

Is there anyone left to hear
My suit? Restore what's mine by right?
Fooled! and so late in your career,
And by a fraud. Well, serve you right!
This whole thing has been criminally mishandled:
Vast outlay, squandered shamefully – a scandal!

Dazzled by daft amours and low-down, common lust –
With my experience?…well it is but just.

Ad spectatores.

But if the shrewd old master chose to be
Mixed up in this infantile absurdity,
And if, in the end, it beat the Devil,
Admit, it can't be all that trivial.

Faust apart, the company played two other plays of Goethe, both to mark anniversaries. *Torquato Tasso* in 1982, the 150th anniversary of his death, and *Clavigo* in 1999, the 250th anniversary of his birth. I have a personal weakness for anniversaries, however meaningless, and they can often be useful in enlisting support of one kind and another from various otherwise quite uninterested parties; both the above dates, incidentally, struck no echo in the rest of the British theatre. Nor has the company attempted similar commemorations in other cases, such as that of Goethe's closest friend and rival Schiller, five of whose plays have been performed in Glasgow, all of them except *Mary Stuart*, I think I am right in saying, for the first time in Britain.

Available in *Faust Parts I and II,* published by Absolute Classics, an imprint of Oberon Books Ltd.

ISBN: 1 870259 11 4

THE ROBBERS
/PASSION AND POLITICS
/DON CARLOS/MARY STUART
/JOAN OF ARC

by Friedrich Schiller

Second to Goethe, and only Goethe, as a poet, Schiller was, if anything, the older man's superior as a playwright, a fact Goethe rather ruefully appreciated. Of the two figures depicted together in the statue group outside the National Theatre at Weimar it is hard to determine just who is handing the laurel wreath to whom; Schiller is turned, seemingly unconcerned, away from the exchange, but with one disengaged hand on the wreath; Goethe's gaze is also fixed on the middle distance, but he is keeping a firm two-handed grip on things. Possibly, too, Goethe's posthumous elevation to National Bard Untouchable might have made him look askance at the personal banning, by Hitler, of Schiller's last tragedy *William Tell*, forbidden in 1941 – he could only have seen it as a mark of failure not to have been banned in such times.

In his first play, *The Robbers*, written when he was only nineteen, Schiller made as sensational a debut as Goethe had with his pseudo-Shakespearean *Goetz*, half a dozen years before: both are important contributions to the "Storm and Stress" movement, coming then into vogue. Telling the story of two brothers, the younger of whom plans the elder's death, the sheer energy of the piece more than makes up for the general scrappiness of construction.

Here the wicked younger brother ruminates on his plan finally to murder the elder.

FRANZ: It is all a matter of how one looks at things; only a fool thinks against his own advantage. A husband has one glass too many, gets the itch – and the result? A human being, probably the last thing in mind during that particular labour of Hercules.

Now I have an itch, and the result will be a human being's death, with more understanding than went to his creating. Most existences result from the heat of a summer afternoon, the sight of rumpled sheets, the pose of some sleeping kitchen slut, or a doused light. If a man's birth is the product of animal compulsion or mere chance, who can call the negation of that birth any great matter? Damn the stupidity of nursemaids and old wives, filling our still soft heads with horror stories, images of fearful punishments, which chill our adult limbs with dread, and block our bold decisions, laying our waking reason in dark chains of superstition. Murder! An inferno of furies flutter around the word. Nature forgot to make one man more, the umbilical cord was not tied off, the father spent the wedding night with the runs – and the whole charade is over. It was something, it will be nothing, and nothing will come of nothing. Man comes from muck, splashes around for awhile in muck, produces muck, and rots away in muck, till he is nothing but muck on the sole of his great-grandson's shoe. And that is the end of the mucky round of the human condition. So, *bon voyage*, brother! Conscience, our gouty splenetic moralist, can haunt hags in bordellos, and usurers on their deathbeds – it'll get no more hearing from me!

Schiller's next play, Passion and Politics*, is his most realistic, and, despite many highly coloured goings-on, his most naturalistic. Set in his own time, it shows the ill-running course of true love between two young people separated by class. Here Ferdinand, the son of the Prime Minister of a principality, has been sent, much against his inclination, to propose marriage to the mistress of the reigning Prince.*

FERDINAND: Dearest Lady, what I am going to tell you now will mitigate my fault and be a sincere apology for the past. I was mistaken in you, my Lady. I expected – I wanted to find you deserving of my contempt. I came here, resolved to insult you and deserve your hatred –

luckier for both of us if that plan had succeeded! I am in love, my Lady – in love with a musician's daughter – Louise Miller. I am aware of what I am embarking on; but even if passion would be wiser to keep silent, the voice of Duty is all the louder – I am the guilty party, I was the first to break in on the golden peace of her innocence – cradle her heart with arrogant hopes and expose it treacherously to passion – you will remind me of my rank – my breeding – my father's principles – but I am in love – the deeper the rift between convention and natural law, between my decision and common prejudice, the higher rise my hopes! We shall see whether the day will be carried by Mankind or by milliners.

Later, with Louise, Ferdinand tries to persuade her to come away with him.

FERDINAND: And my hopes have risen. My father has been provoked. He will be training his whole artillery on us. He will force me to play the inhuman son. I shall no longer feel responsible for my filial duty. Rage and despair will compel me to reveal the secret of his murderous crime. The son will hand the father over to the hangman. The danger is at its height – it was essential it should be for my love to make its great leap. Listen, Louise, – a thought as great and daring as my love forces its way into my soul – you, Louise, and me, and Love – that is a circle that includes all Heaven? Or do you still need a fourth element? (…) If we have no further demands to make of the world, why should we sue for its applause? Why dare where there is nothing to win and everything to lose? Will those eyes not sparkle as brilliantly, whether mirrored in the Rhine, or the Elbe, or the Baltic Sea? My country is where Louise loves me. Your footprints in the savage desert sands hold more for me than the cathedral in my own land. Should we miss the splendour of the cities? Wherever we were, Louise, a sun would rise and set – dramas beside which the liveliest flight of Art pales. If we no longer serve God in a temple, night will fall with captivating excitement, the inconstant moon will preach repentance to us, and a devout congregation of stars shall pray with us. Shall we exhaust ourselves in talking of love? – one of Louise's smiles will last us for centuries, and the dream of life will be over long before I have been able to fathom this tear.

Schiller's next departure was the sort of play he was to write for the rest of his career, a historical tragedy in verse. It constantly astonishes how he was able to renew his means of expression in a medium in which he was so mysteriously apt. From what is apparently a standing start, he proceeds like a sleepwalker, from the heightened prose of The Robbers *(and, incidentally, of Fiesco's* Conspiracy*) to the realistic fluency of* Passion and Politics, *and straight on to a fully-fledged mastery of blank verse in* Don Carlos, *developing what Thomas Mann has called "the most brilliant, rhetorically fascinating style that was ever created in Germany, maybe in the whole world".* Don Carlos *was originally over 6000 lines long – for comparison,* Hamlet, *God knows a long enough evening, comes in at 3750 – and, even after extensive later revision, Schiller only managed to cut about a thousand lines. Whatever his mastery of the theatre, brevity was not part of it. Still, as Max Reinhardt famously remarked: "What you cut can't flop."*

A difficulty with the play is deciding who is the principal character. Despite the title, both the King and the marquis Posa could well fit the bill. Here, King Philip II, at the climax of his royal isolation, wonders whether there can be any genuinely disinterested affection felt for him.

KING PHILIP: Oh, now, give me a man, good Providence.
  Much I have had from you already. Now
  Give me a man. You – you are alone,
  Your eyes examine what is hidden from
  Our sight. I ask you, now, give me a friend;
  For I am not, as you, omniscient.

The helpers whom you had appointed for me,
You know well what they are to me. What they
Deserved of me, they have been paid for, by me.
Their petty vices, kept in check, have served
My turn, just as your tempests cleanse the world.
Now I need truth – and digging for its source
In the dark mud of error and delusion
Is not the fate of Kings. Oh, give me now
That rare man whose heart is clear and open,
Whose spirit shines bright through impartial eyes;
Let him help me find the truth. If I
Shake out the lots, among the thousands who
Flutter about the sun-disc of the Crown,
Guide me to find the one.

Reads in a notebook.

Names – only names
Are written here, no mention even of
Whatever merit they may have to thank
For earning them a place here on this list –
And what is quicker to forget than gratitude?
Yet on the other list I see that every
Last misdemeanour has been noted down.
But why? That is not good. Does vengeance need
Aides-memoire of this kind? Count Egmont? why
Is he down here? – his victory at St-Quentin
Is long ago eclipsed. To the dead with him!
(*Reads on.*) The Marquis of Posa. Posa? Posa? I
Can barely call the man to mind – and yet
I see his name is underlined here – twice.
Surely an indication that I had
Intended great things for him. Can this be?
This man has kept his distance from my presence
All this time? Has he kept out of sight
Of his royal debtor? By God, then he is
The only man in the whole hemisphere
Of my dominions who does not need me!

If he were greedy or ambitious, he
Would long ago have knelt before the throne.
Should I chance this eccentric? One who can
Do without me, may bring me the Truth.

The King sends for Posa, and asks him why he wishes to leave the royal service.

POSA: I am – I must confess, Sire,
    Not, at this moment, quite prepared to dress
    In terms appropriate to a subject, what
    I have thought as a citizen of the world.
    For at the time, Sire, when I severed all
    Connection with the Crown, I did not think
    Myself obliged by the necessity
    Of giving it my reasons for so doing.
    (…) Were I to take the time to do so –
    I would need a lifetime. But if you deny me
    that favour, I will disclose the truth. My choice
    Lies between incurring your displeasure
    And your contempt: and if I must decide,
    I should prefer to leave you thinking me
    A criminal rather than a fool…
    I cannot be the servant of a prince.
    I do not wish to cheat the buyer, Sire –
    If you do me the honour to employ me,
    The terms of that employment would lay down
    What I should do. You need my arm in battle,
    My head in council – and the right, true end
    Of all my actions would not be the actions
    Themselves, but the approval they might find
    Before the throne. But for me, however,
    Right conduct has its own essential virtue.
    This happiness the monarch sows, through me,
    I can create alone, and I would feel
    A joy there, and a freedom of decision,
    Where here it could be nothing more than duty.
    Can that be what you want? Could you endure

A strange creator's hand in your creation?
Am I to descend to be the chisel
Where I can be the sculptor? What I feel
Is love for all Mankind – in monarchies
I may love no one other than myself.
(…) What Your Majesty
Means, through my agency, to spread abroad –
Is it human happiness? And is
That the same happiness that I would wish
Disinterestedly to give Mankind?
That sort of happiness would make a king
Tremble upon his throne – royal *Politik*
Creates another kind of happiness,
One that the Crown is rich enough to bestow
And which will silence rising aspirations
Within the hearts of men. Upon the coinage
It strikes the face of Truth, the only truth
That it can tolerate; all other stamps
That are not like it must be rooted out.
But is what benefits the Crown enough
For me too? Can I love my brother, and
Hire out that love to dispossess my brother?
Can I be certain of his happiness –
Before he is allowed to think? Sire, do not choose me
To sow a happiness that you have minted.
I must refuse to deal in such a coinage.
I cannot be the servant of a prince.

Posa is finally shot on the King's orders on a false suspicion of having treasonous relations with the Netherlanders. He dies in Carlos's arms. Philip enters, and tries to recall his son to his duty; but Carlos refuses to be reconciled.

DON CARLOS: Oh, pardon me,
You who lie bleeding there, if I profane
Our secret, telling it before such ears.
But this great connoisseur of men would die
Of shame to think his greybeard's wisdom

Could have been trumped by the acuteness of
A boy! Sire, we were brothers! Tied together
By a far nobler bond than Nature forges!
The whole course of his life was love – and love
For me the whole cause of his noble death.
He was *mine,* while *you* were bragging of
His reverence for you, and while his quick
Eloquence mocked your proud, unwieldy mind.
You thought you could control him – and you were
Yourself the docile tool of his high schemes.
It was his friendship that contrived my being here,
A prisoner. The letter to the Prince of Orange
Was to save me – the first lie of his life!
Oh, God! To save me, he embraced the death
He suffered. All your favour you had heaped
Upon him – but he died for me. Your heart
And friendship you imposed upon him. Your sceptre
Was a toy that he threw down – and died for me!
And was it possible that you could give
Credence to such a clumsy lie? How much
Contempt he must have felt for you, when he
Took you in with such mountebankery!
You who were paying court to gain his friendship
And failed that simple test! No – that was not
For you. No – that was not a man for you.
He realised that himself, when he rejected
You along with all crowns. But the fine
Stringed instrument was crushed in your iron fist.
There was nothing you could do, but kill him.
(…) You who stand round, who are struck dumb with horror
And with astonishment – must not condemn
The young man who speaks to his king and father
In such a way – look here! He died for me!
Do you have tears? does blood, not molten brass
Flow through your veins? Look there! Do not condemn me!
Perhaps you wait to see how this unnatural story
Is going to end? Here is my sword. You are

My King once more. Do you imagine I
Fear your revenge? Murder me too, just as
You murdered the noblest man that ever lived
My life is forfeited. I know. What is
Life to me now? I here and now renounce
Everything that awaits me in this world.
Go among strangers. Seek a son with them.
Here lie my empires.

By now, Schiller was more interested in writing scenes for two (or more) actors rather than just monologues, however stirring. Big speeches are still there, in plenty, but they only attain their full value when taken together with the surrounding dialogue. Mary Stuart, *for example, contains possibly his best duet, the scene, historically fictitious, between the two queens, Elizabeth and Mary, a real virtuoso display. By the end of it, Elizabeth, convinced of the need to dispose of her rival, soliloquises on the subject.*

ELIZABETH: The slavery of service to the people!
    Humiliating servitude! How tired I am
    Of flattering an idol I despise!
    When shall this head that wears a crown lie easy?
    Defer to their opinions? Fawn on them
    For praise, a stinking mob who would prefer
    To clap a mountebank? No one's a king
    Who still must please the world, but only he
    Who need not ask for any man's approval
    I've practised justice, scorned the arbitrary
    Ways of tyrants all my life, and why?
    Only to find, the moment violence is
    Inevitable, then my hands are tied.
    The example that I gave myself condemns me.
    Were I a tyrant like my elder sister
    Mary, my predecessor on my throne,
    I could shed royal blood without a voice
    Being raised in criticism. But did I
    Make the choice of justice willingly?
    Necessity, which sways the will of kings,

Can sometimes prompt a virtuous decision.
I am surrounded by my enemies;
Only my people's love preserves my crown.
The continental powers conspire my ruin:
The Pope hurls down anathema on my head:
France has betrayed me with the Judas kiss
Of brotherhood, and, out to sea, the Spaniard
Wages an open, fierce war of destruction.
So here I stand, a weak, defenceless woman,
Fighting against a world in arms. I must
Cover the nakedness of my claim with virtues,
Conceal the blemish which my father gave me
At birth – faint hope of that! The malice of
My enemies strips me bare, confronts me with
That eternal threatening spectre, Mary Stuart.
This fear must have an end. Her head shall fall.
I shall have peace. She is my nemesis.
Wherever I have planted joy or hope,
I find this snake of Hell across my path.
She tears my lover from me, steals my bridegroom.
All the disasters that bedevil me,
Are all called *Mary Stuart.* Once she is dead
I shall be free as the air upon the mountains.
The scorn as her glance fell on me, as if
The lightning should have struck me where I stood!
But she is powerless, I have the better weapons.
One fatal stroke and you will be no more.

Goes quickly to the table and seizes the pen.

You call me bastard, you unhappy wretch?
I am one only while you live and breathe.
All doubt surrounding my own royal birth
Will disappear the moment you do too.
The bed where I was born becomes legitimate
The moment England need not choose between us.

*No one who survives a tragedy can be the hero of it, and that rule
holds here. Death scenes could well form an anthology on their own,*

though it might prove gloomy reading. Schiller takes the plunge in fine style, and never lets us down, either in this or in his later work. It is hard, though, to extract a self-sufficient chunk from a scene which depends for its value on its cumulative effect. As Mary finally makes to go, after receiving Communion, after leaving her possessions, and taking farewell of her few remaining adherents, she sees the man who was once in love with her, but chose finally to go back to Elizabeth, and her strength deserts her for a second. He catches her, and she looks at him for a few moments in silence.

MARY: Lord Leicester, you have kept your word. You promised
    Your arm to lead me from this prison, and
    Now you see, I have it.
    Nor, Leicester, was it freedom only that
    I wished to owe to you. You were to make
    My freedom dear to me. I wanted my
    New life to be so happy in your love.
    And now that I must bid this world farewell,
    Become a blessed spirit, far removed
    From the temptations of an earthly love,
    I can confess to you without a blush
    This weakness which I conquered, Leicester.
    Farewell, and, if you can, fare happily.
    You vied for the affection of two queens;
    A tender, loving heart, which you disdained,
    Betrayed, to win a proud one. Kneel to it.
    May your reward not prove your punishment.
    Farewell! – now I have nothing left on earth.

In Joan of Arc, *Schiller, despite having become a professor of history at the University of Jena, played faster and looser with the historical facts than ever before. Whatever we do not know about Joan, we do know she was burnt at the stake, after a long and complicated, but minutely reported trial. In* The Maid of Orleans – *the play's original title, changed by us in Glasgow after finding that nobody in the theatre seemed to have an idea who was meant by it – Schiller has Joan fall in love with an English soldier she is on the brink of killing, and find her death in the thick of her last victory; but what else is martyrdom for a saint?*

Here she is in a rain-drenched forest, on the run from both French and English, accused of witchcraft, and accompanied only by a childhood friend and suitor, who asks why she submitted to the charge without trying to justify herself.

JOAN: Could I deserve to be God's messenger
    And not give blind obedience to His will?
    Nor am I quite as wretched as you think.
    I suffer want, but that is no disaster
    For one of my rank: I'm exiled, an outcast,
    But in the wilderness I have learned to know
    Myself. It was when the glare of honours shone
    About me that my heart was in such conflict.
    When I seemed to be envied in the world,
    That was the time when I was most unhappy.
    Now I am cured, and this great storm in Nature,
    That threatened an end to all things, is my friend.
    It has cleansed the world and me: peace is within me.
    Come what will, I feel no further weakness. (…)
    He who sent this confusion will dissolve it.
    The fruit of Destiny falls when it is ripe!
    A day will come to vindicate me, when
    All those who cast me out and slandered me
    Will be aware of what they did in madness,
    And then the tears will flow for my sad fate. (…)
    All you can see of things is what you see:
    Your sight is still made dim by bonds of earth.
    I have seen immortality face to face.
    God marks the fall of every hair from every head.
    Look over there, the sun is going down.
    As sure as it will rise again tomorrow,
    The day of Truth will just as surely dawn.

English SOLDIERS enter and capture her.

Englishmen, do not let me escape alive
Out of your hands. You must have your revenge!
Take out your swords and plunge them in my heart,
Then drag my lifeless body to the feet
Of your commanding officer. Remember,
I was the one who killed your bravest men,
Who had no pity for any one of you,
Who shed whole rivers of English blood, who took
Away from all those brave, heroic English boys
The happy day when they could go back home!
Now take your bloody vengeance! Kill me now,
Now that you have me; you may not always see me
As weak as this… (…)
Holy and terrible one, hard is your hand.
Am I cast out forever from your grace?
No angel comes, and miracles have an end:
Heaven's gates are shut, God turns away His face

From her prison, where she is chained, she prays.

Hear me, oh, God, in my hour of most need!
To you in Heaven I send my soul in prayer.
You can make cobwebs strong as great ships' cables;
To your omnipotence it is a trifle
To make these iron fetters thin as cobwebs –
If you so will, these chains will fall away,
The prison walls divide – you gave your aid
To Samson, when he lay in chains, and blinded,
Bearing his proud enemies' bitter scorn –
Trusting in you, he grasped the pillars of
His prison, strained and brought it down in ruin!

*Her chains fall away and she flies out to the battle. Later, mortally
wounded, she is in the French camp.*

And am I really back with my own people?
And not an outcast any more? And not despised?
They do not curse me, they look at me kindly.

Yes now I see it all again, distinctly!
That is my King! And that is France's flag!
But I don't see *my* flag – where has it gone?
I must not come without my flag. It was
Given in trust to me by my great master:
I have to lay it down before his throne:
I can do this, since I was true to it.

The flag is handed to her.

Look! Do you see the rainbow in the sky?
Heaven is opening its golden gates.
She stands in glory amid the angelic choir,
Her ever-living Son held to her breast:
Now she holds out her arms to me, and smiles.
What's happening to me? Clouds lift me up –
My heavy armour's changing – I am on wings –
I rise – up – earth falls away so fast –
The pain is short, the joy is everlasting!

There does seem to be rather a lot of Schiller, but of all the more immediately accessible European playwrights, he seems to me to be the most severely neglected in Britain. Now that the National Theatre has had some success with *Don Carlos* perhaps this exile will end. The trouble with the English-speaking theatre is that they hold a trump card with Shakespeare. Whoever is imported is inevitably and unfavourably compared to him, and discarded as second-rate at best.

Available in *Schiller, Five Plays: The Robbers, Passion and Politics, Don Carlos, Mary Stuary, Joan of Arc,* published by Absolute Classics, an imprint of Oberon Books Ltd.

ISBN: 1 84002 036 9

THE SOLDIERS

by Jakob Lenz

A figure not unconnected with Goethe is Jakob Lenz, Goethe's
junior by a mere three years, but obsessed by the solar system
revolving around the man who, since writing *Werther*, was the
most famous author in Europe. Eventually he pursued Goethe
to Weimar, where his eccentric behaviour made him impossible.
His best work is *The Soldiers*, which the company presented at
the Edinburgh Festival in 1993.

*In the final scene, the Commanding Officer proposes a scheme to
prevent the inevitable ruination of young girls by the soldiers, which,
rather like Swift's "modest proposal" that Irish famine could be cured
by having Irish women eat their babies, almost convinces us that it
might work.*

COLONEL: Have you set eyes on the unhappy pair? It put
　　ten years on me. And that something of that sort should
　　happen in my corps! But – Madame! – what can one do?
　　The hand of Heaven hangs over certain people – I'll
　　pay the man's debts and a thousand talers on top. Then
　　I shall see what I can do, through the villain's father, for
　　the family he has ruined – morally and financially.

　　The only advice I can think of for the wretched victim is
　　for her to enter a convent. Her honour is lost, no man
　　could marry her without shame – even though she
　　maintains she resisted the advances of that damned
　　gamekeeper. Were I the Governor, Madame, the fellow
　　would hang…

　　Your tears do you credit, Madame. They affect me as
　　well. Why, indeed, should I not shed tears, I who have to
　　fight and if need be die for my country, having to see a
　　citizen of it and his whole family plunged into
　　irreparable ruin by one of my own subordinates? The
　　consequences of enforced celibacy among soldiers. But
　　how can it be helped? You know, of course, Madame,

that even Homer said that a good husband makes a bad soldier. And experience confirms the view.

A particular thought has always struck me whenever I have read the story of Andromeda. I see the army as a monster to whom from time to time an unfortunate female must be sacrificed so that the other husbands and daughters may be spared.

The King must endow a nursery of soldiers' women; they would of course have to understand that they must give up all the exalted ideas young women entertain about permanent relationships. They would need to be Amazons. As I see it, one noble idea balances the other – the delicacy of female honour against the thought of martyrdom for the state.

Of course, the King would have to do his best to make this condition both brilliant and creditable, in exchange, he would economise on the expense of recruiting, and any children resulting would belong to him. If only someone could be found to promote the idea at Court! I could find sources of support for him. The defenders of the nation would become the good fortune of the nation; the external security of the land would not annihilate the internal; and, in a society until now thrown by us into disorder, peace, prosperity and happiness would join in a single embrace.

Available in *Lenz, Three Plays: The Soldiers, The New Menoza, The Tutor,* published by Absolute Classics, an imprint of Oberon Books Ltd.

ISBN: 1 870259 33 5

THE REPRESENTATIVE

by Rolf Hochhuth

Rolf Hochhuth, born in 1931, has been compared to Schiller for various reasons (humanism, scope, historical grasp, and, it must be admitted, length) but in his first play, *The Representative*, an examination of the actions of Pope Pius XII during World War II, with special reference to his non-intervention in the slaughter of European Jewry, he delivered the most important dramatic statement of the second half of the last century. The emotive power of the domestic scenes, along with the apocalyptic visions of the Holocaust, is balanced by the intensity of the scenes of political argument, of which the central scene of the play, the audience with the Pope in the Vatican, provides the high point.

Here Pius, besieged by several of his ministers, including the young priest Riccardo, begging for his intervention to save the lives of the persecuted by denouncing Hitler, answers his critics with precision and detachment.

PIUS: Certainly this reign of terror against the Jews is

disagreeable,

but we must not allow it to incense us so
that we forget the obligations
which the Germans will have to honour
in the very near future
as protectors of Rome.
Germany must remain viable,
capable of maintaining an independent existence,
not only for the preservation of the Eastern frontiers,
but also to preserve the balance of power in Europe.
The balance of the Continent
is more important than a unity
which hardly corresponds to the old tribal pattern.
On the few occasions that God has caused the rivers of

Europe

to flow in one direction, in one bed:

then the stream has swollen to a torrent
sweeping aside and flooding the old order.
So under Philip II, under Napoleon, under Hitler.
No, each land must have its own stream,
its own directions, limits and frontiers:
that is both healthier, and easier to control.
Alliances, to be sure – but never unity.
What was God thinking of,
when in the winter of '39,
he prevented London and Paris
from supporting Finland in her war with Moscow,
as had been planned?
It had been planned, then nothing came of it.
At that moment, hardly noticed,
the fate of the world was decided:
France and England against Stalin – *that*
would have brought Hitler, who knew even then
that he would have to break with Russia,
to the side of Britain. Under Hitler's leadership
the Continent could
have emerged from the struggle united.
Great Britain would have preserved her Empire.
Why did God not want this?
Why did He let it come to this,
that the West is now tearing itself to pieces?
For a long time we could see no sense in it
but today we know that
Hitler, as World Conqueror,
would subjugate everything, *everything*, and us as well.
He is therefore only to be tolerated,
if he barely survives.
That hour too was God's hour.
The Lord decided to leave us unhurt.
God be praised… We must finish;
our beloved congregation is awaiting us.
It is our wish to urge forward the canonisation
of Innocent XI.

It is most important to us
that great precursor of ours should once more enter
the field of vision of the thinking European.
Under his leadership Christendom formed
an alliance to make a stand against the Turks.
God grant this new aggression from the East
will founder in its turn, because Europe
has recognised in time that in the presence
of this threat she must
bury her internal squabbles.

He makes as if to go, then, after a few steps, when he realises that the FONTANAS, father and son, are standing in his way, he continues.

And pray, beloved in the Lord,
for the Jews, of whom many
will soon be standing before the face of God.

The Representative is published by Oberon Books Ltd.
ISBN: 1 870259 39 4

INTO THAT DARKNESS

by Gitta Sereny

Rather than a speech of generalised horror, I would include one speech from a play using an adaptation of Gitta Sereny's book *Into That Darkness*, an account of the commandant of Treblinka extermination camp, Franz Stangl.

The second half, the speech of the NCO, is included to round off the particular gruesomeness of the story and provide a contrast to the first half.

STANGL: You asked me a while ago, whether there was anything I enjoyed. Beyond my specific assignment, I enjoyed human relations.

GITTA stares at him in disbelief.

I *did* have contact with the work-Jews. Quite friendly relations. The one I talked to most was Blau…him and his wife. I don't know what his profession had been; business I think of some sort. I made him the cook in the lower camp. He knew I would help if I could. He was Austrian. One day he came to my office mid-morning and stood to attention and asked for permission to speak. He looked very worried. I said "Of course, Blau, what is it?" He said his eighty-year-old father had arrived on that morning's transport. Could I do anything? I said; "Blau, you really must understand, a man of eighty…" He said quickly yes of course he understood, but could he have permission for his father to go to the Lazarett and not the gas chambers.

The Lazarett was a roofless shell, with a red cross painted on the front of it. Ostensibly a clinic, it was in reality no more than alternative place for murder. Behind the façade was a low earth wall in front of a pit. After being helped to undress, the old and sick, instead of being gassed, would be made to stand on the wall, and would be shot in the back of the neck, to fall into the permanently burning pit.

Blau asked to take his father there, and first to the kitchens to give him a meal. I said "Go and do what you think best, Blau. Officially I know nothing, but unofficially you can tell the Kapo guard I said it was all right." In the afternoon, he came back, with tears in his eyes and, standing to attention again, said "Herr Hauptsturmfuehrer, I want to thank you. I gave my father a meal. And I've have just taken him to the Lazarett – it's all over. Thank you very much." I said "Well, Blau, there's no need to thank me, none whatever, but of course, if you *want* to thank me, you may."

GITTA: (*Hoarse.*) What happened to Blau and his wife?

STANGL: (*Vague.*) I don't know.

FRANZ SUCHOMEL: (*An NCO in the camp.*) Oh, Blau. He was Chief Kapo to begin with. He'd known Stangl in Austria. Stangl made no secret of it. He'd been a horse-trader or cattle or something. He told me about arriving in Treblinka. He saw Stangl and threw his arms around him. He said Stangl told him "I'm going to appoint you Chief Kapo: help me now and I'll see you survive this. And after the war I'll get you a farm in Poland." Of course he was hated – he collaborated – naturally they hated and feared him. He behaved as if he wanted to outdo the Ukrainians, swinging his whip and shouting, I suppose he did it to survive: who am I to accuse him? Or blame him? Then he asked to be relieved, on medical grounds, heart flutters or something. He and his wife were made to cook for the Jews. The wife was a good cook. After the uprising in the camp, they were among the hundred or so left over, to be evacuated to Sobibor. I heard those hundred were to be shot next day. I warned Blau. I just asked if he had any poison. He understood. They died that day. Better than being shot.

THE LAST DAYS OF MANKIND

by Karl Kraus

Of all plays on the subject of war, recent or otherwise, the most telling, as well as the most voluminous is surely Karl Kraus's *The Last Days of Mankind*, which the company performed at the Edinburgh Festival in 1983, forming part of the Festival's theme of Vienna in the early twentieth century.

Kraus's preface to Last Days *might as well stand for a speech on its own.*

A performance of this play, which would, if computed in terrestrial terms, last for ten evenings, is meant for a theatre on Mars. Earthly theatre-goers could not stand it, for it is blood of their blood, and its material comes from those unreal, unthinkable years, inaccessible to any memory, any waking consciousness, preserved only in a dream of blood, in which the tragedy of Mankind was played out by figures in an operetta –

The action, over a hundred scenes and infernos, is impossible, fragmented and without heroes, just as that other action was. The unkindest actions reported here really happened. The unlikeliest conversations are here reported word for word, the most glaring inventions are quotations – even the Emperor's most-quoted utterance on the war: "It was not what I meant", to invent which would, we must admit, have been well nigh impossible.

None of this gives anyone the right to regard this tragic carnival as a local affair. Far worse than the outrage of the war, is the outrage of those who want to hear no more about it – they can tolerate the fact that it is, but not that it *was*.

An early scene takes place in the Vienna Foreign Office, where a minister is on the telephone to the German Ambassador.

MINISTER: Third class funeral – absolutely, Excellency – Excellency need have no fear – His Highness took the initiative at once – mm?

No, no reigning monarchs – or relations – of course – mm?

No, a Russian Grand Duke was actually ready to leave, thank God we got to him in time.

Demanding explanations – that there won't be war in the end – mm?

Yes, from England as well. – no, nobody, not a soul at Court – just the ambassadors and so forth – absolutely – only a selection of them, the ones one simply cannot refuse – carefully sieved – order of importance – lack of space…

My God, the small chapel…

Absolutely, bitter disappointment – no official participation by the Army – I beg your pardon, Excellency? Funeral Third Class.

Non-Smoker? Ha ha ha very good, I must tell HH. HH will split his sides. Apropos, has Your Excellency heard the shameless suggestion made by his Chancellery yet? That we should be responsible not just for the transport of the coffins and his wife to the station, but also for the private burial. In Arstetten…isn't it…unheard of – our brief goes no further than the family vault.

HH took the initiative at once, of course – told them they should be jolly glad they're getting the coffins taken to the station. The rest is the business of the municipal funeral directors.

Of course, as far as I was concerned, I was against it from the very first, bringing the body of that ghastly little woman by the same train…

Countess Chotek...the Archduchess, well, the
Archduke's wife – but there, HH has a good heart...

And then, Excellency, the Emperor Intervened, and what
can one do? Still, at least he has been able to arrange for
her coffin to be exposed a step lower than her husband's
in the Cathedral...

No, indeed, it will not be pleasant at the station
tomorrow still at least no crowds mm?

I beg your pardon, ah yes, the papers. Fully instructed.
Be no trouble. Watchword, no pomp and circumstance,
just silent grief or what have you...

Couple of entertainment places inquired... whether they
should continue performances. Told them no official
court mourning has been ordered yet and they should
trust their own judgment and taste and what that'll be
like you may well imagine, ah yes...

But my God one can't begrudge the people a little fun in
these hard times – live and let live – 'course o'course –
not just us – whole kingdom mm?

The Attaché asked a police official why he hadn't
arrested one of the assassins, and got told to mind his
own business...

The police at Sarajevo simply did their duty, neither
more nor less –

How many of them? HH took the initiative at once with
their Minister of the Interior – all precautions had been
taken already – six for the Archduke's personal
protection – surely more than enough – I beg your
pardon?

The Foreign Office is in a taking? Absolutely – the best
possible excuse – at last, at last, mm? But of course the
Germans will pull us out of it.

That's it, we're for peace, but not for peace at any price –
ah, no, Excellency, no question of leave, alas, goes
without saying, no fears on that score – arrange
everything – most grateful – thanks – Excellency –
servant...

*Through the whole play ran the character of the "grumbler", clearly
intended as an author's mouthpiece, and known by us as "Kraus the
Grouse", commenting endlessly on the happenings, conversations,
newspaper quotations, telephone calls, and everything that showed
the war in all its grotesque horror. Towards the end of what, even on
a good night, was a marathon evening of not much under four hours,
the entire cast left the Viennese café in which the action had so far
taken place, and before the surrealist chaos of the final descent into
madness and destruction of the world, the single figure of Kraus,
who had been at his table the whole time, spoke up one last time with
the voice of Reason.*

KRAUS: The wish to establish the exact time needed to
transform a growing tree into a newspaper encouraged
the proprietor of a paper factory in the Harz district to
make an interesting experiment. At 7.34 a.m. he had
three trees growing in a forest near the factory cut down,
and after their bark had been removed, they were taken
to the pulping plant. The transformation of the trunks
into a mass of liquid pulp was so fast that the first roll of
newsprint left the press by 9.30. This roll was taken
immediately by lorry to the newspaper office four
kilometres away, and by 11 a.m. the newspaper was
being sold on the streets. It had therefore required a
period of only three hours twenty-five minutes for the
public to be able to read the latest news on material from
a tree on whose branches birds had been singing that
morning.

Voices crying "Extra. Late Extraaa!" KRAUS looks at his watch.

Five o'clock then. There is the answer. The echo of my
bloody insanity, and no other sound comes to me from

battered Creation but that sound, in which the ten million dead and dying accuse me for still being alive.

What did you die for?

If you had all together possessed the imagination to notice the contrasts you would have saved your skins.

Had you known, at the moment of your sacrifice, known of the profit, which grows despite – no – with the sacrifice, battening on it. For never, in this indecisive war of the machines, has there been such a godless profit in war, and you, victors or vanquished, have lost that war, which has brought profit only to your murderers.

And for that you lay for four years in filth and wet, for that the letters were delayed that should have reached you, the book held up that should have comforted you. They wanted you to stay alive, for they had not yet stolen enough on their stock markets, not lied enough in their newspapers, not tortured Mankind enough, they had not yet pursued to its end this whole tragic carnival, in which men died under the eyes of women war correspondents, and butchers were made honorary doctors of philosophy, not yet taken it through to the last dance and the morning of repentance.

Oh, if one could have come through this adventure, if one could, through some divine retribution, receive the strength to call the eternally surviving ringleaders of world crimes, to account, one by one, to lock them in their churches, and there, as they did to the Serbian peasants, have every tenth man draw the lot of death.

And then, not to kill them – no – but to slap them in the face and say to them: what, did you not know, you children, that the consequences of declaring war, among the million possibilities of horror and ignominy, are also that children have no milk, horses no grain, that far from shot and shell a man may die of methyl alcohol poisoning, if that is part of the war plan of the profiteers?

Did you not measure the misery of a single hour of the yearlong sufferings of a prisoner?

A single sigh of longing, of love defiled, torn apart, butchered?

And did you never notice how the tragedy became a farce, how modern monstrosities, existing simultaneously beside a mania for old ways, made it an operetta, one of those appalling new-style operettas, where the text is an insult, and the music a torture?

Did you overlook the fact that once you have put all Mankind into uniform, they must endlessly salute one another? Hysteria protected by technology, overpowered Nature, and paper commanded weapons. We were crippled by the rotary presses before we fell victims to the cannons.

In the end was the Word. The Word that killed the spirit could only proceed to give birth to the Deed.

Weaklings became strong, and drove us under the wheels of Progress. And that was the doing of the Press alone, to defile the world with its whoredoms. Not that the press set the machinery of death in motion – but that it hollowed out our hearts, until we could no longer imagine how things would be. And because we could no longer imagine them, they had to be. Because if we could have imagined them, they could not be: that is its war guilt.

And the horseman of the Apocalypse, he whom I saw raging through the land a decade before he spoke, spoke unto the press. "He runneth full speed ahead through every highway and byway. His toothbrush moustache reaches from North to South, and his forelock from the rising of the sun to the setting thereof. And to the horseman power was given, to banish peace from the earth, that men would fall upon one another to slay them. I saw him as the beast with ten horns and seven heads and his mouth was as the jaws of a lion. And men fell down and worshipped the beast, saying 'Who is like unto the beast? And who may stand against him?' and a mouth was given unto him to speak great things." And because of him we fell, and because of the Whore of Babylon, who spoke to us in all the tongues of the world, to convince us we were one another's foes, and that there must be war.

And you, the sacrifices, who did not defend yourselves against the orders to die. Will you not rise, dead, from your holes in the earth, to call these vermin to account? Ask them what they have done to you.

What they did during the winters you spent in Galicia. What they did that night when orders telephoned to your units received no answer.

For all was quiet at the front.

Only later did they see how you were still standing there, bravely, shoulder to shoulder, rifles at the ready. For you belonged neither to those who went over to the enemy, nor to those who fled: you stayed at your posts. Before you the enemy, behind you the fatherland, and above you the constant stars.

It is not your dying, but what you had to experience that I wish to revenge on all those who forced you to it.

I have shaped them into shadows, which they are, to which their semblance wished to give life.

I have stripped the flesh from off their bones.

But I have given flesh and motion to the stupidity of their thoughts, the wickedness of their feelings, the terrible rhythm of their futility. My ear has caught the sounds of what they did, my eye the gestures of what they said, and my voice has done nothing but quote them, preserving the keynote for future time. And if future time will not hear, then let whatever being is above them hear. For it may be to be feared, that a future, sprung from the loins of such a terrible present, may, despite the greater distance, dispense with a greater strength of understanding. Worse than all the ignominies of war is that ignominy of Mankind, not to wish to know about war: they will accept that war exists, but not that it existed. Then let that spirit that has mercy on the fallen, even if it has denied itself contact with Humanity for all time, let it receive the keynote of this time, the echo of my own bloody insanity, through which I too am guilty.

And let me speak to the yet unknowing world
How these things came about. So shall you hear
Of carnal, bloody and unnatural acts,
Of accidental judgments, casual slaughters,
Of deaths put on by cunning, and forced cause
And in the upshot, purposes mistook,
Fallen on the inventors' heads. All this I can
Truly deliver.

Of that I always shall have cause to speak.
And let this stand for an atonement.
All their blood was only ink in the end –
Now the writing will be in blood. This is the war.

VOICES: E-x-t-r-a . L-a-t-e – e-x-t-r-a.

The rest of the play is taken up with a huge epilogue The Last Night. *While technically unstageable – stage directions like "twelve thousand horses come up out of the sea" put one on one's mettle – it is nevertheless a necessary finale to what has gone before. Here, a chorus of ravens flies croaking round a mountain of unburied bodies.*

CHORUS: Ravens find nutritious feeding
　　Wherever men for honour die,

Where so many men lie bleeding
Keeping up the food supply.

For the dead you hardly grieve,
Generals, fellow-marauders,
Since it is proof positive
That the fools obeyed your orders.

Who minds if you lose a battle?
You, and we, will always win.
While the men who die like cattle
Keep us all in pro-te-in.

As you gorge the night away,
Half a million dead dismissed.
We feast, in our usual way,
Off the casualty list.

Since you rescued us from hunger,
Generals, accept our thanks:
We don't feel it any longer,
Since we joined up in the ranks.

An old SERBIAN digs his own grave.

We stood around the empty store,
The soldiers yelled at us and swore.
They took all we had tried to save,
And now they make me dig my grave.
They put my children against a wall;
Before my face they took them all.
My goods are burned, burned is my land,
I dig my grave with my own hand.
My children call – Lord, let me rise
And be with them in Paradise.

A wounded SOLDIER speaks.

Mother, I feel the pressure of your hand
Setting me free from night and Vaterland.
What happiness, to breathe my native air!

The thunder of the night has rolled away.
What did they want from me? I cannot say.
Oh, Mother, it is morning! God is there.

Finally, the voices from Mars announce the end of the world, and press the button. Through the ensuing mayhem we hear a single voice – who? – speaking the Emperor's line quoted at the beginning of the play: "It was not what I meant."

DER ROSENKAVALIER (Libretto)

by Hugo von Hofmannsthal

In tandem with *Last Days* at the Edinburgh Festival, the company performed the libretto by Hugo von Hofmannsthal for the opera *Der Rosenkavalier*, almost certainly the only opera book to have been given unaltered as a straight play. Inevitably the high romantic moments would have benefited from a musical accompaniment, and conversely the comic moments probably fared better for being shorn of theirs.

Here is an aria of Baron Ochs auf Lerchenau, the villain of the piece, or more accurately, the buffoon.

OCHS: *Parole d'honneur,*
    Nothing to beat the pleasures of the chase.
    All seasons, days and hours, not one
    Where one may not
    Filch an arrow from the blind god's quiver.
    That's why a man is not a woodcock or a stag,
    But the Lord of Creation – because he is not forced,
    Saving Your Highness' presence, to obey the calendar.
    Par exemple, every schoolboy knows
    The month of May to be propitious for the business.
    But let me tell yer,
    Better still June, July – and August!
    There's nights for you!
    At home we've such a rush of girls from Bohemia
    Come across for the harvest,
    And come across for a good deal else as well.
    I often keep two or three of 'em in the house
    Till November, then pack 'em off back home.
    And what a mixture it is –
    Young, sonsy, Bohemian girls,
    Sweet and stacked,
    Along of our true Germanic stock,
    Sharp and tart as a mountain wine –

What a brew that makes.
And everywhere there's something happening,
A larking and a rustling at lattices,
A slipping in together, a lying down together,
And everywhere a singing,
And a swinging of hips,
And a milking
And a mowing,
And a paddling and a splashing in the streams and the
                                        horsetroughs!
Ah, could I just be like the late Jupiter of happy memory,
In a thousand disguises,
Something for everyone!
As many different ways to take a woman,
As there are women to be taken by them.
I know my way about the landscape, God be Praised!

MASKERADE

by Mikhail Yurievich Lermontov

Another curiosity, to set beside numerous others, was Lermontov's *Maskerade*, which we performed in autumn 1976, a continuation of the high-flown, romantic style exemplified in such things as *Vautrin* the following year. Banned by the Tsar, for not very clear reasons – maybe for showing members of the nobility in an unflattering light – it had to wait for a century, before the great director Meyerhold planned a production, of unexampled magnificence, which had its dress rehearsal, the theatrical event of the decade, on the twenty-fifth of February 1917, the day when the first shots of the Revolution were fired in St Petersburg.

The story concerns a dissolute nobleman, Arbenin, who is rapidly being reformed by his young wife, Nina. Social intrigues, however, persuade him she is unfaithful to him; he poisons her at a ball (with ice-cream) and goes mad with remorse. Alongside Lermontov's view of the corrupt society of the 1830s, there is the mysterious figure of a stranger, who is seen as Arbenin's nemesis, a sort of demonic judge, simultaneously driving him to crime and punishing him for it. Plenty of room for turmoil here, one would think, and rightly. Here Arbenin advises the Prince, who has been losing heavily at cards, on his future.

ARBENIN: I've known this place a long time. I can remember the speechless excitement with which I used to watch the spinning of the wheel of fortune: for no reason, one would be lucky, and another ruined, also for no reason. I would watch them, and feel like the wheel itself, indifferent. I used to see young men, oh so full of hopes and feelings, happy in their ignorance of life, eager, ardent souls whose only previous object had been love, and they would burn up, like that, as I watched… and now it would seem I was watching it all over again.

Listen to me. You can do one of two things only. Either you vow never to touch a card again for the rest of your life, or you can go back to the table this minute, but remember, if you go back, you go back in order to win, and to win here, you have to abandon everything else: family, friends, honour. You must learn to dissect your own abilities and character, without passion.

You must learn to read clearly the thoughts and impulses on the faces of people you hardly know.

You must spend years learning to control the movements of your hands and the movements of your features.

You must spend the days in practice and the nights in gambling.

You must never know a moment's freedom from torment, and no one must guess that you are in any way tormented.

You must not betray your fear when you meet your equals in art and skill across the same table.

You must live with the knowledge that at any moment your luck may run out, and in the most humiliating way imaginable.

You must accept with the same impassivity the names they will call you, not blushing even when accused of the worst possible things.

And you must learn to despise – to despise everything: and the man who despises everything can love – Nothing. Yes, there is a price on all this, you see.

Having won back all the money the Prince had lost, Arbenin now suspects the Prince of having an affair with his wife. Although he has promised her not to gamble any more, he allows a slightly sinister friend, Kazarin, to talk him round.

KAZARIN: I'm delighted to hear you say you're a happily married man, though I can't pretend I'm not sorry you're married at all. I just remember the old days, when we were together, on the town. Lying in bed all morning, reminiscing about the events of the night before. Then dinner at Raoul's, the best he could provide, cut glass sparkling into life as the wine was poured, and talk, talk, talk, and more jokes than you could ever remember, or even count. Then on to the theatre – I still feel a shiver of pleasure when I think how we used to stand in the wings waving to the ballerinas…it's true, isn't it, that in the old days everything was better – and cheaper? And after the play we flew like arrows to a friend's house, up the stairs, and there would be the game already in progress, with mountains of gold scattered all over the table: some faces flushed and hectic, others pale as corpses. Our sitting down would be the signal for the battle to begin in earnest.

There at the table, we breathe another air.
Thought, sense and feeling join to make a man.
Armies of passions, legions of sensations,
Tramp through your soul, and time and time again,
The restless mind is wound up like a spring
By some gigantic thought,
And if your skill and nerve and strategy
And cunning can outwit your enemy
And bend the laws of chance, there are for you
No further worlds to conquer:
Beside you, Bonaparte himself becomes
A pitiful and slightly shabby clown.

Arbenin now uses his skill to make it appear the Prince has been cheating, and takes his revenge.

ARBENIN: Highness, if you wish to kill me, you had better do it at once, before what courage you have evaporates.

I am a gambler. Come, come now, Prince, no tears, childhood is over. I could blow your head off at thirty yards: I am tolerably in practice. Or I could have killed you this afternoon. Why do you suppose I did not do so?

You couldn't bear to be obligated to me, and you chose to discharge that obligation to me, by making me a stock figure of fun. Well, on that occasion the choice of weapons surely was mine, and you see the weapon I have chosen. No one will think the worse of me for refusing to fight with a seducer and a cheat. And if they do, then you must understand that I do not care. I am no longer concerned with rules – all that ended the day I discovered what you had done to me. You not only made me your enemy, you unwittingly decided what sort of enemy I was going to be. We should be careful in our choice of friends, but a lot more careful in our choice of enemies.

There, that is all I have to say. From now on, you will be able to watch yourself becoming harder and colder, as all the feelings of love and nobility in you gradually flicker and die. It is closing time: the fairground is locking its gates, and you are outside. May I wish you a long life and excellent health.

BRAND

by Henrik Ibsen

In *Brand*, Ibsen depicts an uncompromising hero-priest, a personification of Norwegian political conscience. His recurring monologues only make their best impression by their cumulative effect in context, but the speech of Agnes, Brand's wife, trying vainly to call back the spirit of their dead child, makes an interlude on its own, regardless of the fact that the succeeding scene shows her forced by her husband to abandon even those small relics of the past in order to find freedom from its tenacity.

AGNES: Shut! Everything is shut! Shut off –
　　Even oblivion is denied me.
　　Tears are forbidden, sighs cut off
　　While they lie half-formed inside me.
　　I must go out: I can't breathe the air
　　In these lonely rooms. But where?
　　Where is "out"? Unrelenting eyes
　　Gaze down at me from lowering skies.
　　Must I leave my heart's ease here?
　　Can I fly from my silent fear?

She listens for a moment at BRAND's door.

　　Reading aloud: he cannot hear.
　　No help or comfort anywhere
　　At Christmas God has too much to do
　　With the rich and happy to listen to
　　A lonely mother's tale of woe.

Going cautiously to the window.

　　If I did draw the shutters back,
　　The light would shine out through the crack
　　And chase night's terrors from his black
　　Sleeping-place. But no, he's not there.
　　Christmas is the children's time:

Perhaps he'll be allowed to come;
Perhaps he is already here!
Wasn't that a child's voice?
Ulf, I don't know what to do!
Your father has shut up the house,
I dare not open it for you.
You're an obedient little boy,
We never did anything to annoy him.
Fly home to Heaven – go back! Fly!
Just don't let them see you cry.
Don't tell them your father locked
You out, when you came and knocked.
It's hard for a little boy like you
To know what grown-ups must go through.
Tell them he sorrows, say he grieves,
Tell them how he picked the leaves
To weave into the wreath, how he
Made it for you. Look! Can you see?

Listens, starts and shakes her head.

I'm dreaming! There's so much to be done
before we meet again, my son.
I must work, silently, to fulfil
His every demand. I'll steel
Myself, stiffen up my will.
But tonight is Christmas, though,
Different from a year ago.
But shh! It is a holy night;
I shall take my treasures out,
relics saved from the shipwreck of
my happiness, impossible
to value, and accessible
only to a mother's love.

Takes various articles out of a chest.

Here are his christening robe and shawl.
And here's his smock – dear God! How sweet

And pretty! How smart he looked in it,
Sitting up in church. And all
His other things, his scarf, the coat
He wore when it was freezing out;
The first time that he put it on,
It was too long – but not for long.
Here are the things I wrapped him in
For making the long journey South…
After I'd put them back again,
I was so tired – tired to death…
Oh, still to possess this treasure
Makes me rich beyond all measure.

Brand is published by Absolute Classics, an imprint of Oberon Books Ltd.

ISBN: 1 870259 27 0

A WASTE OF TIME

by Marcel Proust

In September 1981, we embarked on what was a watershed production, and a marathon – a performance of Proust's *A la Recherche du Temps Perdu*. It was originally planned as a serial, lasting a whole season, but finally moderation prevailed and it was reduced to a single evening – a pretty long one, indeed, but single – with the slightly challenging title of *A Waste of Time*, though no critic rose to the provocation – it seems there are barriers which even they will not cross. Clearly, in the boiling-down of a three and a half thousand page novel, with almost that number of characters, all existing in complicated relationships with each other, there was not much room left for indulgent speechifying. However, here is a bit of Mlle de Villeparisis, the high-born aunt of at least three of the major characters, giving the hero a bit of advice.

MLLE DE VILLEPARISIS: Sainte-Beuve used to say character develops in war, talent in peace. Or maybe it was the other way around. Probably stolen anyway, he was a fearful magpie. But peace you certainly have and pleasure in writing comes from writing. I'm sure you must just keep moving. The son of one of my friends is in a very similar way to you. He resigned from the Quai d'Orsay to devote himself to writing. A small talent, but he has had no reason to regret the decision. He published last year – some years older than you of course – a book on "On the Sense of the Infinite on the Western Shore of Lake Nyanza", and has just followed it up with a very pointed, sometimes too pointed, little thing on "The Use of the Repeating Rifle in the Bulgarian Army". One can't say he has reached the pinnacle of his profession, but his name has been mentioned, and not unfavourably, at the Academy of Moral Sciences. So you see, success is not entirely the province of agitators, misfits and trouble-makers, as so often seems to be the case.

(…)

Balance and judgment are what you must strive for, Marcel. They will give you a mind which will give your life more happiness, more dignity than the more liberal refinements which bring so many artists to such suffering and to a disrepute which I am sure your parents would not wish for you. Like those novels of Stendhal you profess to admire so. I assure you it would have surprised him. My father, who knew him quite well, told me he was appallingly vulgar, but good company and not a bit conceited about his books. Balzac paid him absurdly extravagant compliments and he just shrugged. But Balzac, whom everybody seems to idolise nowadays, was never really received in the society he attempted to describe with such wildly improbable results. As for Hugo, I am afraid such extravagance was only ever accepted as literature after he struck his not entirely disinterested bargain with the dangerous errors of the Socialists.

But this eternal talk of "society" is most unpalatable. "Society" is a word never used by those who are supposed to belong to it. I remember Vigny – now there's a dull writer, if you will – introducing himself to me with: "I am the Comte de Vigny." As if a gentleman would have said such a thing. One either is a Comte, or one is not, and that's all there is to it. Our social personalities are created by what others think of us. One must either be in "society" or be an enemy of it – what is of no use at all is to envy it, or try to please it. Still, the aristocracy in these days, what does it add up to? To my mind, a man who doesn't work, doesn't count.

Earlier, Marcel, the hero, encounters a formidable social figure, the Baron de Charlus, the grandeur of whose position is matched only by his arrogance in insisting on it, and the dubiousness of whose sexual tastes is matched only by his dedication to indulging them. He is here making some sort of set for Marcel.

BARON DE CHARLUS: I see you have taken to going into society. You must do me the pleasure of coming to see me. There are complications, though: I am seldom at home. You would have to write. I understand that you took part this morning in one of those orgies my nephew has with that actress. If you have any influence with him you would do better to point out the pain he is causing his poor mother, his aunt – his great-aunt, and, indeed, all of us, by dragging the name of Guermantes in the mud.

There is a lot I could do for you, but I ask myself whether you are worth the trouble I should have to take with you. Well, are you? With the usual lack of consideration common to people of your age, you are liable to say things which would put an unbridgeable gap between us. What you said just now, on the other hand, makes me want to do a great deal for you. I shall be leaving soon. Come with me.

I too have only just arrived. I am surprised to see you at this idiotic tea-party, and more so, and less pleasantly, to see you would prefer to remain at it. A waste of time. It is clear you find it hard to distinguish between benefits. Make your farewells.

Irresolute to the last, I see. The demands of Society can only be damaging to you at present, warp your character, such as it is. And be particularly careful about your choice of friends. Keep mistresses, if your family don't object, and if that is to your taste, that's hardly my concern, you young scamp. Is that a moustache you're trying to grow? My nephew Robert is quite suitable as a companion for you. He can do nothing for you, no matter, for the future I am sufficient, but he presents no serious drawback. Yes, I think you would be worth my time and trouble. I should need to see you every day, should need proofs or at any rate, indications, of loyalty, and discretion, which you look as if you might be capable of. You stand at the parting of the ways, my young friend, like Hercules, though sadly for you, and perhaps for me, without his muscular development.

Shall we walk?

Charlus, on quite another walk, encounters Jupien, a tailor, acquainted with Marcel's family, with whom he, Charlus, strikes up a relationship, which goes through numerous changes from pick-up to pimp and finally to nursemaid. Here is a moment when the nature of the acquaintanceship is about to change.

JUPIEN: Grow a beard? Disgusting! Do you know anything about the man who sells chestnuts at the corner, no, not the one on the left, he's repulsive, but the big, dark boy? And the chemist opposite has the most delectable delivery boy. What about him?

You could find out. You could find your way in such circles with a deftness denied to one of my rank: great bodies move slowly. I'm sure you have a gift.

Yes, as you say, you have shown me. But that is over between us, now that we have spoken of serious subjects. It is unfortunate, as I should have been glad to accommodate you another time. But you could do me great services, by acting as my – agent, yes an excellent idea. I feel a new man.

You will point out to me bus-conductors, sleeping-car attendants, page-boys, among whom I shall move like Haroun al Raschid, incognito through the sleeping city, without being subject to those dismal, solitary homeward journeys from out-of-town stations of little interest,

where I have just seen Cherubinos met by their families,
Bartolos and Marcellinas to a man, those families which
I was witless enough never to suspect as being among
the many defects of character of those I had pursued with
such unrewarded dedication and expenditure of time,
while they, all unaware, had been sharing a back-rest in
the tram with someone, myself, to whose acquaintance
their mothers would have preferred for them that of a
blind leper with a time-bomb in his hand.

Later, Jupien explains to Marcel the way things have progressed.

JUPIEN: Monsieur, I am...well, surprised is hardly the
word, to see you here...perhaps you didn't know...that
I was in business. Oh, yes, but it doesn't bring in all you
might think. I have respectable boarders too, though of
course I couldn't make out on them alone. Prices are
going up every day, and scrap metal all needed for the
war. The price of chain, I can't tell you. No, the truth is,
I only took the house to keep him interested in his old
age. Save him being bored: you see he's really a big
baby. Even with everything he wants here, he still isn't
above running after little adventures, and I'm afraid little
adventures of the kind he likes may get him into a little
bother some day. He offered so much money to a boy
the other day, the boy thought he wanted him to be a
spy, and nearly went to the police. So relieved he was
when he found he was only being asked to surrender his
body and not betray his country. Not that it's any more
moral, just less dangerous. And certainly easier. Not that
I have scruples about the job. I like it. It's to my taste.
And it's not a crime to enjoy one's work and get money
for it, not that I've heard.

*Twenty years on from that production have brought various indications
of progress, in the course of some two hundred productions in what
had become three auditoria. Progress, however, does not mean
invalidating what has gone before, and I hope that these speeches will*

continue to interest for a few years more, and, more importantly, that they may encourage people to read the whole plays from which they come, all of which could do with a further airing, rather than sinking back into the dusty storage boxes from which the Citizens' Company briefly rescued them.

Finally, it only remains for me to thank the members of the Citizens' Company, in particular the following actors, for whom these speeches were written, and who first spoke the lines from the stage, for their talent, patience and understanding. In no particular order, like the speeches, but in all cases with, at the very least, respect, admiration and affection…

Gerard Murphy, David Hayman. Julia Blalock, Joyce Redman, Glenda Jackson, Diana Rigg, Barbara Jefford, Andrew Wilde, Eamonn Walker, Ciaran Hinds, Garry Cooper, Mark Lewis, Yolanda Vasquez, Jonathan Coyne, Robin Sneller, Paul Albertson, Giles Havergal, Andrew Woodall, Benedict Bates, Fidelis Morgan, Ann Mitchell, Charon Bourke, Derwent Watson, Henry Ian Cusick, Roberta Taylor, Gary Oldman, Kim Thomson, Robin Hooper, Jane Bertish

And in memoriam,

Tristram Jellinek, John Breck